74

IRRESISTIBLE FORCE

DISABILITY SPORT IN CANADA

IAN GREGSON

POLESTAR

BOOK PUBLISHERS

Polestar Book Publishers acknowledges the ongoing financial support of The Canada Council; the British Columbia Ministry of Small Business, Tourism and Culture through the BC Arts Council; and the Government of Canada through the Book Publishing Industry Development Program (BPIDP).

Cover and interior design by Jim Brennan.
Printed and bound in Canada.

Canadian Cataloguing in Publication Data
Gregson, Ian, 1962-
Irresistible force

ISBN 1-896095-49-6

I. Sports for the handicapped—Canada. 2. Physically handicapped athletes—
Biography. 3. Handicapped—Canada—Recreation. I. Title
GV709.3.G73 1998   796'.0456   C99-910617-9

Library of Congress Catalogue Number: 99-63537

Polestar Book Publishers
P.O. Box 5238, Station B
Victoria, British Columbia
Canada
V8R 6N4
http://mypage.direct.ca/p/polestar/

In the United States:
Polestar Book Publishers
P.O. Box 468
Custer, WA
USA
98240-0468

54321

Canada

Acknowledgements

This book was inspired by a conversation with the late Merv Oveson and Vic Cue. Thanks are due to Gerry York, Mike Armstrong, Tim Frick and all the athletes, coaches and organizers who agreed to be interviewed. The completion of a project of this magnitude is not without its limitations. Interviews and research were performed on a limited budget. Thank you, Chris Bourne, for providing valuable assistance.

Finally, I wish to acknowledge the invaluable support of my family, who muddled through the ups and downs of writing a book with me. We finished our first marathon! To my wife Sharon and our children Nick, Ben, Emily and Elizabeth: thank you for sticking with me all the way to the end.

Dedication

This book is dedicated to Michael Johnston and Gary Collins Simpson, two extraordinary athletes who left us long before their time was up.

CONTENTS

by Patrick Jarvis

A s I listened to the waves slapping the ancient beach in India, it occurred to me just how far we have come. These thoughts about distance travelled had nothing to do with the considerable miles I had journeyed to reach India; rather, they were thoughts about the progress made by Canadians in the realm of sport for athletes with a disability.

I had just finished reading the manuscript of Ian Gregson's *Irresistible Force*, which recounts a significant portion of the journey made by athletes, volunteers, coaches and others involved with disability sport. In a relatively brief period of time, this movement has shed its cloak of sympathy for "those less fortunate" while gaining the respect and dignity that come with athletic accomplishment. Reading this book entrenched my thoughts: How far we have come; and how far we have to go!

I have known Ian Gregson for approximately ten years, first when I was his teammate in athletics and later when I was a volunteer with the Canadian Amputee Sport Association. It would be misleading for me to say that I am in complete agreement with all the views that Ian holds, but over the years I have come to appreciate his ability to challenge the status quo on various issues. Some of Ian's strongly held views come to light in this work and I hope that they may add fuel to current debates within the disability sport community. Indeed, the strong opinions of other individuals within this community are also presented — including divergent or conflicting points of view. I am a proponent of such passionate debate. The exchange of disparate views, as long as it is respectful, helps clarify issues and provide guidance for the growth and evolution of a movement.

The world of disability sport is rife with complex issues. Its environment engenders strong beliefs from people with powerful convictions about the value of sport. The plethora of acronyms are as bewildering as the convoluted issues that are the focus of discussion among those involved in the movement. *Irresistible Force* provides insight into these issues as well as an historical framework of people and organizations who have been central to the growth of the movement. It would be wrong to say that this book offers the panacea of issue resolution. Rather, it serves to inform and educate. And, most important, it serves to acknowledge the efforts of numerous deserving individuals.

This book touches on both the highs and the lows of the disability sport movement. It offers insight into some of the tremendous successes of athletes with a disability as well as some of the disturbing situations the athletes have endured. Many of the athletes' stories show the relative simplicity of overcoming physical obstacles as compared to the difficulty of surmounting attitudinal barriers. Athletes with a disability and their supporters have fought diligently for recognition of their talents and abilities and, most of all, for equality of opportunity. Much of their success is due to the efforts of dedicated people — and to the fact that equality of opportunity is an idea whose time has come.

Books chronicling the achievements of Canadian athletes and sports organizations abound — but none captures the triumphs of Canadians involved in disability sport. There have been so many "trail-blazers" — outstanding individuals with a disability who have endeavored to achieve equity in sport. Almost all of them remain virtually unrecognized within Canadian society and the history of sport. *Irresistible Force* redresses this imbalance by acknowledging the accomplishments of these unsung trail-blazers. It is a work long overdue.

O ne rainy Vancouver night after a fund disbursement meeting of the Gordie Howe Disabled Athletes Foundation, I had a conversation with fellow participants Vic Cue and Merv Oveson. Actually, it was a one-sided event: Merv and Vic reminisced about the early days and I simply listened and took it all in.

As I drove home that night I thought to myself, "How far we have come in such a short time!" I mused over the revelation that, in the space of my own lifetime, people with disabilities have progressed from being virtual "shut-ins" to people performing on the world stage at the Olympic and Paralympic events. I thought about how, even 50 or 100 years ago, the opportunities for people with disabilities to participate in sports simply did not exist. I imagined how difficult it must have been for the likes of Stan Stronge and Doug Mowatt to form Canada's first wheelchair basketball team in the days long before government support. It occurred to me that Stan and Doug were no longer with us and we have lost the stories they could have told. I thought of my good friend Gerry York who, aged seventy-eight, is still deeply involved in BC Blind Sports.

How sad, I thought, that no one had ever documented the experiences of Stan or Doug. I realized that I still had an opportunity to tell the stories of Gerry, Vic, Merv and many others who had played pivotal roles in the development of disability sport in Canada. How difficult could it be? I had lots of experience interviewing people from my years as a radio station DJ. I had a good knowledge of "who's who" in the Canadian disability sport movement, both from my years as a Paralympic athlete and as chair of the BC Sport and Fitness Council for the Disabled. I had also gained writing experience on disability issues with magazines such as *Explore, Disability Today, Truck Logger* and *Freedom Magazine*.

Vancouver Sun sports reporter Wendy Long had recently published a book, *Celebrating Excellence*, on Canadian women in sport. I surmised that the publisher who had produced such a book would be open to my proposal for a similar book on disability sport. For this reason, I approached Michelle Benjamin at Polestar Book Publishers. She was interested in my idea and we soon met and settled on an agreement. My first book was out of the starting blocks.

In the end, it has been my experience as an athlete and volunteer, as well as my thoughts on that rainy Vancouver night, that affected how this book came together. The words and pictures in *Irresistible Force* record what it was like in the "old" days and, by presenting profiles of today's promising athletes, show how far we have come. Within these pages you will meet with controversy, dissension, opposing views and frustration. You will also meet with accomplishment, against-the-odds bravado and a uniquely Canadian perspective on issues that are of concern to millions of people around the world every day of their lives. Perhaps most important, you will meet the people themselves — the incredible athletes of yesterday and today. Although many names and achievements are, by necessity, not included here, I believe that *Irresistible Force* does represent a great start.

The development of sport and recreation for people with disabilities in Canada is an ongoing process. Since the end of the Second World War, people with disabilities have made great strides in gaining recognition as contributing citizens. One of those great strides has been in sport and recreation. In fact, one could say that sport and recreation have directly affected the social advancement of people with disabilities. After all, there are few opportunities for people with disabilities to excel in front of large audiences. Participating in sport has allowed many people with disabilities to express themselves publicly.

Fifty years ago, very few of us dreamed that, one day, people with what were then called "life-inhibiting injuries" would show the world their athletic skill by participating in demonstration events at the Olympics. Back then, no one had conceived of the Paralympic movement, nor that it would develop into one of the world's largest sport bodies. And certainly no one would have believed that Canada would play a major role in the development of sport and recreation for people with a disability.

In almost all the interviews I conducted for this book I asked, "With hindsight, what could we have done better?" Some athletes and volunteers believed that things had been done right the first time; some believed that we have been held back by bureaucracy; some believed that we still have a long way to go. Everyone agreed on one thing: that over the last 50 years Canada has developed its own unique method of organizing sport for people with disabilities. Sometimes this "delivery system" has worked and sometimes it has failed, but it has rarely stayed the same for long. Success certainly can be measured in the number of medals received by Canadian athletes at the most recent Paralympic event, which took place in February 1998; it can just as easily be measured in the number of Canadians with disabilities currently active in sport and recreation. Whichever benchmark we use, it is clear that we have made remarkable progress over the years.

In the 1990s, sport for people with disabilities has faced — and continues to face — its greatest challenge. We have achieved so much that our competition can no longer be disability based; instead, it must be based on the sport itself. There are numerous sport-specific models currently in use — the model most often cited is Swim Canada's attempt to include swimmers with disabilities within its own ranks. However, although Swim Canada's program encourages swimmers with disabilities at the "elite" level, it is not designed to directly encourage swimmers at regional or provincial levels, and these swimmers remain under the jurisdiction of the existing disability-based programs. In order to exist, such programs must receive the blessing of the local sport organizations and the federal government. Too often we have seen federal governments initiate a plan with proper consultation and research only to have the plan fall apart when no one seems to consider it worthwhile. While the integration of athletes with disabilities into sports with non-disabled athletes is a stated governmental goal, this integration has sometimes been achieved without consultation with non-disability sports organizations. No wonder these organizations become defensive!

The positive result of the advances of the past years is that it now appears that people with disabilities are moving toward true integration with the non-disability sport community. This will have its pitfalls as well as its rewards, but hopefully the benefits will outweigh the costs. In the end — as our history shows us — it is we, the people with disabilities, who must steer our destiny towards our own goals and rewards.

AN OVERVIEW OF DISABILTY SPORTS IN CANADA

by Wendy Long

In the early days of February 1999, the international soccer world was rocked by the news that English coach Glenn Hoddle had been fired. Normally such an event is of interest only to folk who follow the sport. But the circumstances surrounding Hoddle's dismissal made for much greater public interest and discussion. The firing of a coach is a common occurrence in sport but it was Hoddle's words, rather than his coaching record, that prompted his downfall. Hoddle was dismissed after the *Times of London* published an interview which included Hoddle's thoughts on reincarnation. The paper reported that Hoddle believed people with a disability were being punished for the sins of a past life.

These remarks were surprising, even shocking, for a culture that, at the end of the twentieth century, has become accustomed to more intelligent and thoughtful words about people with a disability. Hoddle said later that he was misquoted and misunderstood. But the incident serves as a warning to anyone who believes that the way is now clear for people with a disability to achieve success and recognition in life — or in any sporting or professional avenue they might choose. Old prejudices and misconceptions remain.

An old adage says that sport is a microcosm of life, and so it is for the athlete with a disability. He or she has more opportunities than peers who competed 30 years ago but is still confronted by media and public perception that his or her activity is "therapy" or "recreation" rather than elite athletic endeavour. Athletes with a disability throughout the world — including many such athletes from Canada — are helping to change those perceptions through their success in competition, their willingness to discuss issues and their commitment to the long and hard training that is the only route to international success. They long ago left behind the notion of sport as simply therapy.

Saskatchewan-born Eugene Reimer was the first Canadian athlete with a disability to truly gain international success. In 1968 he broke discus and club throw world records in Tel Aviv at what were then called the Wheelchair Olympics (the event that would eventually be renamed the Paralympics). Four years later at the Heidelberg Wheelchair Olympics, Reimer won gold medals in discus and pentathlon, feats that earned him recognition as Canada's outstanding male athlete for 1972. Two years later he received the Order of Canada. On the track, in marathon racing and through his Man in Motion world tour, wheelchair athlete Rick Hansen personified courage and ability. By the end of his journey, the term "disabled" seemed a poor and inaccurate adjective with which to describe the man. In 1981, Terry Fox captured the attention of the world with his Marathon of Hope for cancer research. That marathon was stopped short in Thunder Bay when Fox was stricken again with cancer. Later, Steve Fonyo embarked on another cross-Canada marathon to raise money for cancer research and he successfully completed the task in May 1985. In recent years, Canadians such as wheelchair athlete Jeff Adams, swimmer Walter Wu and thrower Ljiljana Ljubisic have served as impressive personal and athletic ambassadors for their country and their respective sports.

While many athletes with a disability have initially taken up sport for social, therapeutic or recreational reasons, for some it was a natural progression to test their limits — to race faster, throw farther and play better. Sport organizations specifically for athletes with a disability came into being at the provincial and national levels as demand for organized programs and coaching increased. For example, Canada's history of excellence in events for disabled skiers began with the formation of the Alberta Amputee Ski Association in 1969. Five years later the first Canadian Disabled Skiing Festival was held at Sunshine Village near Banff, Alberta, and Canada subsequently sent athletes to the World Disabled Skiing Championships in France. The Canadian Association for Disabled Skiing (CADS) was established in 1976 and over the next several years the national body worked to form provincial divisions. In addition to national organizations for individual sports, there are also several national sport associations designed to serve specific groups in the disabled community — organizations such as the Canadian Blind Sports Association (CBSA) and the Canadian Amputee Sports Association (CASA). Internationally there are also major sporting events for specific disability groups and specific sports, such as the world blind sports championships, the Special Olympics and the world wheelchair basketball championships.

Since 1960, the Paralympic Games have evolved to become the pinnacle of athletic competition for athletes with a disability, just as the Olympic Games serve as the highest career goal for able-bodied competitors. The seed of what would become the Paralympics was sown in 1948 with the Games for People with Spinal Cord Injuries, held at Stoke Mandeville Hospital in Aylesbury, England. The event was organized by Dr. Ludwig Guttmann as part of a rehabilitation program for persons with spinal injuries. The concept blossomed, and twelve years later in Rome (also the site of the 1960 Summer Olympics) 400 athletes representing 23 countries took part in what is regarded as the first Paralympics, although it featured only wheelchair athletes. It wasn't until the 1976 Paralympics in Toronto, which complemented the Summer Olympic Games in Montreal, that blind, wheelchair and amputee athletes made up the 2,700 competitors from 42 countries and the event became officially known as the Paralympics. The first Winter Paralympic Games were also held in 1976, at Ornskoldsvik, Sweden. In 1996, the 10th Paralympic Summer Games in Atlanta attracted 4,000 athletes from 125 countries competing in events from track-and-field to swimming, from judo to equestrian. The 1998 Games in Nagano, Japan marked the first time the winter event had been held outside Europe. These games, held two weeks after the Winter Olympics in the same city, featured 1,000 athletes from 30 countries.

The International Paralympic Committee (IPC) administers and oversees the event in cooperation with member national governing bodies such as the Canadian Paralympic Committee (CPC). In recent years, athletes and disabled sport organizations have discussed the goal of melding the Olympics and the Paralympics into one grand event celebrating all the world's best athletes rather than having separate games for able-bodied and disabled competitors. But can the Olympics and the Paralympics — which in recent years have been held one after the other in the same host city and utilizing the same sport and athlete village facilities — ever meld into one great athletic showcase?

Since the 1984 Olympics in Los Angeles the games have featured wheelchair races as part of the track and field program, although the races have had demonstration rather than full-medal status. In 1992 an important perceptual link was forged when Spanish archer Antonio Rebollo served as a key figure at the opening ceremonies for the Summer Olympics in Barcelona. Rebollo, stricken with polio as a baby, took up archery at age 22 and had won medals in Paralympic Games competition. Rebollo's task at the Olympic opening ceremony was to light the Olympic flame by shooting a flaming arrow into the cauldron at one end of the stadium. The scene marked one of the most dramatic flame lighting episodes in Olympic history and the fact that an accomplished Paralympian had played such a critical role in the "big show" for able-bodied competitors opened the doors for discussion of some integration and collaboration. Closer to home, the 1999 Canada Winter Games in Newfoundland showed that greater steps are being taken to recognize athletes with a disability and to include them as part of the games with their able-bodied counterparts. At the opening ceremonies, cross-country skier Francine Lemire, a gold medallist at the 1988 Paralympics in Austria, lit the torch to begin the games. The games also included wheelchair basketball as a full-medal sport.

Still, there remains a concern that athletes with a disability deserve a separate event to showcase their particular sports and talents. "We don't want to lose the identity of the Paralympic Games," stated IPC chair Robert Steadward while addressing the question of a merger of Olympic and Paralympic games prior to the Paralympics in Atlanta. "I think we also need to look at whether there is a site that can host at least 20,000 athletes at one time." His question is crucial given that the International Olympic Committee is already seeking to somehow curb the number of athletes taking part in the Summer Olympics. Scheduling, security, accommodation, transportation and rising costs already make each Olympic Games an organizational challenge verging on a nightmare.

There is no doubt that a vast chasm exists between the Olympics and Paralympics — indeed, between able-bodied and disabled sport — in terms of media and public exposure. The Olympic Games traditionally draw hordes of media from around the world while the Paralympics receive far less attention — particularly from Canadian media, which have tended to depart *en masse* from the Olympics, leaving few reporters to document the heroics of Paralympic athletes. Without media exposure, athletes with a disability do not have a chance to capture the interest of the public and are not potential candidates when sponsors are searching for a sport or athlete to support.

Yet the world of disabled sports can be confusing for journalists accustomed to following popular able-bodied sports such as professional hockey. It is human nature to stick with what we know best and, at least initially, the disability classifications for athletes in a variety of sports may appear unwieldy and confusing — it is not surprising that members of the general population mistake the terms B1, B2 and B3 for vitamin groups rather than visual acuity classifications. But sports such as sledge hockey and goalball, designed specifically as events for competitors with a disability, can be as exciting and compelling as able-bodied events. The challenge remains to entice members of the media and general public to watch and learn.

Sport, regardless of the discipline, is about people — not only about their winning and losing but also about why they put in the effort, how they cope with disappointment, their joy in a task achieved, the lessons learned in trying. Entertainment and inspiration aren't the sole domain of the professional hockey or basketball player. The human spirit abounds not only in the Stanley Cup final but among the chairs and wheels on the basketball court, between guide runner and blind athlete.

We must frown on the absurd comments made by Glenn Hoddle and worry about prejudices that may linger in people's hearts. So, too, must we rejoice in the sometimes celebrated, often unsung, exploits of all people with a disability who contribute so much of their talent, commitment and determination to the world of sport and to the world in general.

PARALYMPIC CATEGORIES OF DISABILITY

The Paralympics are the pinnacle of sport for athletes with a disability and are held in the same venues as the Olympic Games (shortly after the Olympics conclude) on the same four-year cycle. There are nine categories of disability for athletes who compete in the Paralympic Games.

Amputees

An amputation refers to a missing limb or portion of a limb. Congenital amputation occurs at birth — a person is born without a limb or parts of a limb. Acquired or traumatic amputation occurs as a result of illness or an accident. Amputations can affect an individual's balance and locomotion. A prosthesis for upper or lower limb amputations helps enhance mobility and limb function.

Cerebral Palsy (CP)

Cerebral palsy is caused by damage to the brain before, during or after birth due to an interruption in the oxygen supply to the brain. CP affects the control of movement and posture. The level of disability varies from no visible signs to multiple signs involving lack of control of facial and limb movements, and speech difficulties.

Les Autres (LA)

This category includes people with polio, muscular dystrophy and spina bifida, and people with locomotor disabilities resulting from injuries to the musculoskeletal or nervous system.

Mental Disability

A mental disability may be congenital (i.e., an individual is born with it) or acquired through an accident or as a result of a disease. Mental disabilities vary considerably. People may be socially mature or socially delayed; gifted in their motor abilities or lagging behind their peers; have low self-esteem or have great personal confidence; have good verbal skills or use a board to communicate. Down syndrome is the most common chromosomal abnormality (a person with Down syndrome has 47 chromosomes rather than 46) resulting in mental disability. This genetic anomaly causes various degrees of developmental delays. The classic physical features of a person with Down syndrome include a round face, short stature, lack of a fold in the eyelids and small fingers.

Muscular Dystrophy

Muscular dystrophy is a genetic disease characterized by progressive muscular weakness and atrophy of the muscle fibres. Paralysis results from the gradual degeneration of arm, shoulder and leg muscles.

Poliomyelitis (Polio)

Polio is a viral infection of the motor cells in the spinal cord that leads to muscular paralysis and atrophy of the muscle or bone. The severity of the infection determines the extent of the neural damage and paralysis. Some muscles are completely hindered, while others are only weakened.

Spina Bifida

Spina bifida is characterized by a developmental buckling of the spine in which one or more of the vertebral arches fail to close completely during gestation. This leaves an opening in the spine that leads to nerve damage and affects muscle function and sensation.

Spinal Cord Injury

Spinal cord injuries result in paralysis that inhibits movement of the lower extremities and all or part of the trunk muscles. The degree of disability from a spinal cord injury depends on where the injury occurred along the spinal cord. In general, the higher the injury on the cord, the less function there is because more muscles are affected. Paraplegics have limited or no function in the lower body. Quadriplegics are affected in both arm and leg movement.

Visual Impairments

Visual impairments can vary in degree and type. An individual can have partial sight or can be completely blind. Some people can only distinguish the difference between light and dark. Others see in a mist or see shapes and specks of light. Still others see nothing at all.

ACRONYMS

CAAMH: Canadian Association for Athletes with a Mental Handicap

CADS: Canadian Association of Disabled Skiiers

CanTRA: Canadian Therapeutic Riding Association

CASA: Canadian Amputee Sports Association

CBSA: Canadian Blind Sports Association

CCPSA: Canadian Cerebral Palsy Sports Association

CFSOD: Canadian Federation of Sports Organizations for the Disabled

COA: Canadian Olympic Association

CPC: Canadian Paralympic Committee

CPU: Canadian Powerlifting Union

CTRA: Canadian Therapeutic Riding Association

CWBA: Canadian Wheelchair Basketball Association

CWSA: Canadian Wheelchair Sports Association

CYA: Canadian Yachting Association

FCA: Federation of Canadian Archers

FITA: Federation of International Target Archery

IAAF: International Amateur Athletic Federation

IPC: International Paralympic Committee

IPF: International Powerlifting Federation

ISMWSF: International Stoke Mandeville Wheelchair Sports Federation

ISOD: International Sport Organization for the Disabled

NCCP: National Coaching Certification Program

NSO: National Sport Organization

PSO: Provincial Sport Organization

SFC: Shooting Federation of Canada

SNC: Swimming Natation Canada

1

The Paralympic Sports and the Athletes

ALPINE SKIING

I n keeping with a long tradition of Canadian success in skiing, Canada's athletes with a disability have continually appeared among the best in world rankings and Paralympics events for skiers.

Jerry Johnston is recognized to be the founding father of skiing events for people with disabilities. While running a ski clinic in Banff, Alberta in the early 1960s, Johnston was approached about teaching people with polio how to ski. The program grew quickly from there. Yet despite its relatively early beginning as a winter sport for people with disabilities, alpine skiing has yet to gain as much prominence as many of the more recently developed summer sports.

One of the unique features of the Canadian Association for Disabled Skiers (CADS) is that it was the first national organization to be sport specific and to include people with different disabilities. At the time of CADS' official creation in 1976, most national sport organizations (NSOs) were developing in the opposite way — as multi-sport, single-disability groups. Today, all major organizations for people with disabilities feature skiing in recreational and competitive programs. Organizations for amputees, the visually impaired, paraplegics, post-polio athletes and those with cerebral palsy all sponsor international alpine ski events at the Canadian Nationals, Paralympics and World Championships.

Today, all major organizations for people with disabilities feature skiing.

There are four disciplines in Alpine Skiing: Downhill, Super Giant Slalom, Giant Slalom and Slalom. Various adaptations exist for the different types of people with disabilities who participate in alpine skiing. Skiers who are blind or partially-sighted ski with a guide who provides the competitor with verbal instructions on his/her direction and slope. Single above-knee amputees (commonly referred to as "three trackers") use a single boot and ski poles adapted to have small skis on each tip. These "outriggers" can be positioned so that they may be used as crutches and also help with lift lines. Skiers who compete standing (one or two skis depending on their disability) may also use outriggers. Double above-knee amputees and paraplegics use a "sit ski," which is similar to a racing wheelchair but is equipped with skis instead of wheels. Among those who have excelled at this form of skiing is Canada's former top wheelchair athlete Daniel Westley, who has transferred his success on the track to the slopes.

■ SPORT HIGHLIGHT

Canada's international success in the 1980s centred around three top amputee skiers: Lana Spreeman, Linda Chyzk and Phil Chew. All three skiers were three trackers and all received top honours in the grand slalom, super G and downhill events. At the 1998 Nagano winter Paralympics, Marnie Winder of Delisle, SK won a bronze medal in the women's slalom, a silver medal in the super G and another bronze in the giant slalom. Stacy Kohut of Calgary was also a triple medallist, placing second in the super G, giant slalom and slalom. Dan Wesley of New Westminster, BC won a gold medal in the men's super G for sit skiiers and a bronze medal in the downhill race. Colette Bourgonje (see profile under "Cross-Country Skiing") and Karolina Wisniewska both won double silver medals, while Mark Ludbrook (see profile) and Ramona Hoh both won a bronze medal.

ATHLETE PROFILE

alan *heaver*

Key Events: Track and field, skiing

Card: uncarded

Classification: A4 summer; ISOD–LW4 IPC winter

Birthdate: 1950

Birthplace: London, England

Current Residence: Vancouver, BC

PHOTO: *Alan Heaver at the Olympics for the Physically Disabled, Holland, 1980.*

■ CAREER HIGHLIGHT

In 1980 made the Canadian national team in track and field, and competed in the pentathlon, receiving a gold medal in this sport at the Olympics for the Physically Disabled in Holland. In 1986 competed for Canada at the winter Paralympics in Innsbruck, Austria, and at the World Championships in Sweden.

Upon immigrating to Canada in 1957, Alan developed his early athletic skills in a number of sports — high-school basketball, hockey, volleyball, swimming, baseball and soccer for the Toronto City juniors. It was in the sport of ice hockey, however, that Alan showed the most promise. Before losing his leg below the knee in 1969, Alan played junior hockey in Toronto and attended college in Ohio on a hockey scholarship. Loss of the limb prevented Alan from joining the Detroit Red Wings after the draft that year. Nonetheless, Alan maintained his interest in hockey and learned to skate using a prosthesis. He was an instructor in several hockey schools in the Toronto area and had the distinction of teaching several players who later went on to join the NHL.

Alan's first introduction to disability sport came through the Ontario Crippled Children's Centre (now the Hugh MacMillan Centre) when he was 23. Alan was involved in the school of orthotics and prosthetics at George Brown University in Toronto and met people who were already involved in disability sport. Shortly thereafter, in 1977, he attended an Ontario regional track meet and "never looked back." Coached by John O'Brian in all track and field disciplines, Alan competed at the Ontario Championships later that year and at the Canada Games for the Physically Disabled the following year, setting most track and field records for below-knee amputees. In 1980 Alan made the Canadian national team and for the next few years competed in the pentathlon (which involved five sports, including swimming). He received a gold medal in this sport at the Canada Games.

As chief orthotist at the Ontario Crippled Children's Centre, Alan was invited to attend a learn-to-ski program at Georgian Peaks in Ontario. He learned to ski as a "three-tracker" as it was widely believed at the time that below-knee amputees were not capable of skiing using a prosthesis. With his athletic background and competitive nature, Alan soon became interested in racing. He entered his first competition at Georgian Peaks for "a lark." On moving to Edmonton in the mid-1980s, Al secured a position on the Canadian national ski team. In 1986 he competed for Canada at the winter Paralympics in Innsbruck, Austria, and at the World Championships in Sweden. "Just making it to the winter Paralympic team was a major highlight competition-wise," he remembers. "That same year I beat Patrick Coufert, who was one of the top b-k [below-knee amputee] skiers in the world at the time."

> *"The media coverage, regardless of medium, is still sadly lacking. There is so little you hear about disability sport competitions."*

Upon wrapping up his skiing career in 1990, Alan turned his attention to furthering his knowledge of orthotics at the Pentlands facility in Vancouver. His achievements include developing a prosthetic ankle for skiers.

In looking back upon his athletic career, Alan remarks, "If you look at the general population of Canada there seems to be more acceptance and appreciation now of how talented athletes with a disability are. The major difference from when I first started competing is in the mentality of the athletes at national and international competitions. Now their goal is to give 110 percent of their heart and soul. Sport has become extremely competitive, the standards are so much higher, the level of excellence is miles ahead of what it was … yet we still have a long way to go."

Being an athlete with a disability has some drawbacks and disappointments, even today, says Alan. "The media coverage, regardless of medium, is still sadly lacking. There is so little you hear about disability sport competitions." Al also voices concern over the limitations of current resources available to athletes with a disability. "I think training centres for coaches, so that they can work with the athletes, still need to be developed and improved upon. Of course the underlying factor behind all this is funding. Athletes still cannot attend all the competitions or training camps of their choice, or obtain proper coaching."

Alan has chosen not to remain involved with disability sport organizations after his retirement as an athlete. "I've not been involved in Canadian disability sport due to the administrative side of things, with all the bullshit and crap that has taken place there," he explains. "There are too many people who have tried heart and soul to change things, but there is still too much deadwood sticking around, which burns most people out. The reason why some organizations fly and others don't is because new people are brought in. They look at things differently and so things gradually change."

Despite his concerns, Alan remains generally optimistic about the value of sports for athletes with a disability. "Competing in sport allowed me to travel and meet lots of different people. Anyone who has this chance should grab hold and take it."

These days Alan takes the direct approach to encourage people with disabilities to become involved in sport. Through his professional work as an orthotist he is ensuring that amputees have prostheses that enable them to do the things they used to do — and more. As Alan Heaver has demonstrated throughout his life, the single-handed and independent-minded approach has its merits.

ATHLETE PROFILE

mark *ludbrook*

Key Events: Skiing (downhill, super G, giant slalom, slalom); swimming

Card: A

Classification: LW4

Birthdate: 19/1/1967

Birthplace: Stoufville, ON

Current Residence: Whistler, BC

■ CAREER HIGHLIGHT

Winter sports: Silver medal at the 1998 Paralympics Nagano, Japan; two silver medals in swimming events at the 1984 Paralympic Games in Los Angeles; Paralympic team member in 1984, 1988, 1992

M ark Ludbrook's athletic career spans almost 17 years, and his athletic accomplishments in both swimming and downhill ski racing have enabled Mark to compete for Canada at both winter and summer Paralympics. When Mark is competing in his favourite sports, his normally relaxed, outgoing personality switches to an intense mode that often leaves fellow competitors scratching their heads in amazement.

Mark's athletic career as an amputee began in 1979. Shortly after losing his leg below the knee, he contacted swimming coach Alan Dean in Aurora, Ontario and began swimming with Alan at St. Andrews College. Technology played a major role in Mark's decision to take up swimming as a full-time sport. His other option was to train in track events, but the lack of technological developments in below-knee prostheses pushed Mark toward the pool. He progressed quickly and attended his first national competition, the Amputee Nationals in Vancouver, in 1980.

During the early 1980s Mark swam with the Newmarket Stingrays, a non-disabled swim club. There were no other swimmers with a disability in the club and the club had certainly never seen an amputee swim before. The other swimmers quickly adjusted to his presence though, and in 1984 Mark competed for Canada at the International Games in New York, winning a bronze medal in the 100 metre freestyle event, a silver in the 200 metre medley relay and a silver in the 4x100 metre freestyle relay. This turned out to be his best-ever performance at the international level.

In 1987 Mark studied at Brock University and trained with the varsity swim team; in 1988 he competed at the Paralympics in Seoul, finishing fourth in three races. After this event, Mark took a year and a half to travel to some of the places he had visited and made friends. His travels included a long stay in Australia.

Upon his arrival back in Toronto in 1990, Mark began work for Rogers Cablesystems as a field service representative. Now that he had a full-time job, Mark found he had hardly any free time for training, and no coach could be expected to schedule sessions around Mark's busy workday.

Mark quit his Toronto job to begin a new sport in Whistler, BC: skiing.

As a result, Mark trained alone. Although he put in the hours, distances and weights, he did not have the finer points of the sport perfected by the time he competed at the 1992 Paralympics in Barcelona. He did not bring home any medals. "The competition in Barcelona was a lot stiffer than ever before," Mark remembers. "If I had been taken in by a coach four months before the competition, I would have done much better in Barcelona." As well, notes Mark, the use of an integrated class system at these games played a significant role in the results for all below-knee amputees.

At the end of 1992 Mark quit his Toronto job to begin a new sport in Whistler, BC: skiing. Mark had always wanted to learn how to ski, but the lack of ski hills in the Toronto area had been a limiting factor. "One of the first things I said to my mother [after losing my leg] was that I'd never be able to ski!" he remembers. "But in Whistler you are surrounded by people who love the sport. We all live for the sport — everyone wants a short summer. There is a lot of moral support here, but not a great amount of financial support."

Mark immediately recognized the limitations of skiing with a conventional prosthesis in the below-knee category. These limitations were clearly evident when Mark competed at his first ski nationals in 1987. There simply wasn't the prosthetic technology to enable skiers like him to maintain control in the sharp turns. Rather than switch to three-track skiing, Mark decided to address the issue of limited prosthetic technology for skiing. The difficulty in prosthetic technology is that each prosthesis is custom built for the individual. An added factor for the downhill skier is the high stress on the prosthesis while skiing. "Technology plays a big part in disabled skiing," explains Mark. "You have to get the lightest and the quickest prosthesis, and the one with the best fit, and you have to customize it to suit your needs. I had to put out $3000 to $4000 for a ski leg." It was at this stage that Mark decided even a customized commercial prosthetic product simply could not suit his athletic needs. He sat down and designed a prosthetic ankle that gave him the range of motion he needed to complete the aggressive turns in the slalom events. "If I want to perform I have to use this ankle," he says.

In 1994 Mark competed at the Canadian Nationals against significant competition from New Zealand, the United States and Japan. Mark garnered a gold in the slalom and two silvers in the super G and downhill races. "The 1994 Nationals really pumped me up," he remembers. "After that I realized I could keep going and make it onto the national team. Even if I didn't make the national team, I still wanted to live in Whistler and ski 100 days out of the year."

At the 1995 Canadian Nationals in Kimberly, Ontario, a new classification system was implemented in which skiers with different levels of amputation could theoretically compete against each other. The new class system involves a "handicapping" factor in which monoskiers, three-trackers and those who compete using two skis can compete in the same event. Back in the "old days," athletes used to win a medal just for turning up. Now, "instead of having the old ten gold medal syndrome, they have cut it down to two," explains Mark. "It used to be anyone could walk away with a gold medal because of the lack of competition in each class — which is great if you are 10 years old, but when you get older you realize you are the only one in your class.

"The new system adds and subtracts times from the skiers [according to disability] in order to work out the result. It was pretty difficult to watch someone perform a slower time and yet receive a gold medal. Still, even though there are a few bugs to be worked out of the system, the principle is sound and the medals are worth more." Mark took home a bronze medal and a silver medal from the Canadian Nationals in that first year, and in 1998 he won a bronze medal in the Nagano Paralympics.

Mark Ludbrook's longtime ambition was to be a medallist in both summer and winter Paralympic Games. Fortunately, neither technology nor reclassification could prevent him from reaching his goal.

ARCHERY

A rchery was one of the sports played at the first recognized sport event for athletes with a disability — the Stoke Mandeville World Wheelchair Games, which took place at Aylesbury, Buckinghamshire, England, in 1948. As a result, archery was considered an essential sport for paraplegics and quadriplegics for many years at the annual Stoke Mandeville Games. Today, although archery is not a very popular sport in Canada, there are groups of archers in various locations across the nation, including Winnipeg, Manitoba and the Variety Village facility for athletes with a disability in Toronto, Ontario.

Archery is a sport where athletes with a disability can compete on an equal basis with non-disabled athletes.

Target archery has been a Paralympic sport for over 30 years. The Paralympic program includes doubles, singles, and team events using the same competition and scoring protocol as utilized in the Olympic games. The official governing body is the Federation Internationale de Tir L'Arc or the Federation of International Target Archery (FITA).

Paralympic competition is limited to athletes with cerebral palsy, spinal injuries and other lower limb impairments, and les autres conditions; however, athletes with other disabilities also enjoy archery. Archers in the Paralympic Games compete in wheelchair and standing classifications.

Archery is a sport where athletes with a locomotor disability can compete on an equal

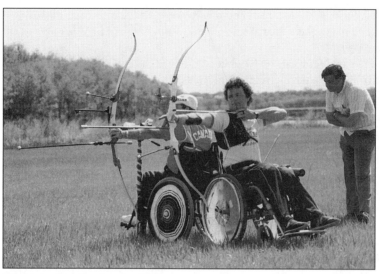

Wheelchair archers competing, circa 1988.

basis with non-disabled athletes. Archers shoot six "sighter" (trial) arrows and 36 arrows at distances varying from 70 to 30 metres for women and 90 to 30 metres for men. The playing field is similar in design to that used by "able-bodied" athletes. The target is a distance of 294 feet (90 meters) away from archer. The maximum target size is 48 inches in diameter (122 centimeters). The target is divided into 10 concentric rings with a golden "bulls eye" or center ring. The rules and scoring protocol are the same as those used in the Olympic games. Points are earned for each arrow striking the target. Archers score ten points if they hit the bulls eye and one point if they hit the outer ring. The closer the archer's arrow lands to the bulls eye, the more points earned.

Paralympic athletes use a recurve bow. Recurve bows are made of wood, graphite, fiberglass or carbon composites. Arrows are either carbon graphite or aluminum. Bow lengths and weights vary considerably. Generally, persons in wheelchairs use a 48-inch bow. Women use a 20 to 30 pound bow, while men use a 30 to 40 pound bow.

Wheelchair archers require no equipment modifications. They do, however, position themselves at a ninety-degree angle from the target and may remove the front armrest to allow increased draw of the bow string. Wheelchair archers are allowed to use seat and back cushions, although there are restrictions on thickness. In general, seat cushions are restricted to 15 centimeters while back cushions are restricted to 5 centimeters.

Non-Paralympic wheelchair athletes may use a wheelchair bow stringer, in which a pole is vertically mounted into the ground near the archers' stand. Two large covered bolts are strategically placed on the pole to allow the archer independence in stringing the bow. Diagrams of this device are available in most adapted sports or adapted physical education texts.

Archers with significant upper extremity disability are allowed to utilize a device to secure the bow to the hand. These devices may be as sophisticated as a universal cuff or as simple as tying or bandaging the bow to the hand of the archer. Additionally, persons with significant upper extremity disability are allowed to have a person nock the arrow onto the bow. However, this person may not give the archer any verbal advice or coaching tips nor may they be disruptive to other competitors.

Archers with bilateral hip disarticulation, or archers with bilateral above-knee amputations with shortness of residual limbs prohibiting the use of prostheses, are allowed to use strapping or a body support from the base of the wheelchair. There are many rules regarding strapping and body support systems; in general, a chest strap can be no wider than 50 millimeters (1.97 inches) and can be placed no less than 110 millimeters (4.33) below the armpit.

Sighting aids that comply with FITA rules may be used when competitors are shooting at

An archer sights a target.

outdoor archery targets. Some of the commonly used adaptations in equipment and techniques are: foot blocks that orient the archer to the target; audible sound source positioned at or behind the target; brightly colored target for persons with partial sight; and balloons on target to provide auditory feedback.

Some archers also use a bow sling, a loose strapping device that is secured to the wrist of the bow hand. This device may be used by persons with mild spasticity or others who have a tendency to drop the bow when they release the string. Some amputees use a prosthesis or terminal device with hook fingers. One end of the device is held by the hook fingers and the other end has a notch that allows the archers to draw the string. Upon full draw, the archer is able to release the arrow with a slight rotation of the prothesis.

Competitions in archery are classified according to four disciplines: outdoor target archery; indoor target archery; field archery (experimental); and ski archery/arcathlon (experimental). The archery classification system uses disability profiles and a numerical calculation of locomotor ability as guidelines. All archers are tested for locomotor abilities and points are given for muscle dysfunction (coordination) and joint mobility. A baseline of 380 points is assigned to able-bodied archers, with full points accorded to arms (190 points), trunk (60 points) and legs (130 points). The minimal disability to be eligible to compete in the Paralympics is a loss of 25 points in the upper limbs or 20 points in the trunk or 15 in the lower limbs — or 25 in total.

Also popular in the 1960s and 1970s was the sport of Dartchery. As the name suggests, Dartchery is a combination of lawn darts and archery. Dartchery was an official Paralympic event for International Stoke Mandeville Wheelchair Sports Federation (ISMWSF) athletes for many years, until disability-specific events became unpopular.

■ SPORT HIGHLIGHT

In 1984, Neroli Fairhall of New Zealand became the first wheelchair athlete to meet eligibility requirements and earn the right to compete in the women's archery competition at the Los Angeles Olympics.

COACH PROFILE

charles j.
drouin

KEY EVENTS: Archery

BIRTH DATE: 14/08/1960 (died 02/99)

BIRTH PLACE: Montreal, QC

CURRENT RESIDENCE: Ottawa, ON

"The biggest barrier is the attitude of some able-bodied event organizers and the condescending attitudes of some officials."

■ CAREER HIGHLIGHT

Coach of the archery team at the VIII Paralympic Games in Seoul, South Korea, 1988

Following is an interview the author conducted with Charles Drouin in June 1998. Sadly, Charles passed away less than a year later, in February 1999.

How, when and where did you first get involved in disability sport?
I first became involved in 1976 when I was a counsellor at a summer camp for children with disabilities in St. Alphonse de Rodriguez, Quebec.

Were there people who inspired you to become involved?
Yes, Roger B. Mondor and Donald Royer, who were involved in wheelchair sports, were inspirational.

What sports and activities besides archery have you been involved in?
I've played racquetball and tennis, and I've also been involved in swimming.

What do you see as your greatest accomplishment in sport?
My greatest moment came during the 1988 Paralympic Games in Seoul, when I was involved in the decision making process with several international federations: the International Stoke Mandeville Wheelchair Sports Federation (ISMWSF), the International Sports Organization for the Disabled (ISOD) and the International Paralympic Committee (IPC).

What do you see as your greatest disappointment?
I continue to be disappointed by the lack of visibility and spectators for disability sports.

Do you have any concerns about the direction of your sport for the future?
Yes. There's an unfortunate tendency to create and promote disability-specific events in archery. In my opinion we should be more in line with able-bodied events.

What is the most significant barrier facing athletes with disabilities at your level of competition?

The biggest barrier is the attitude of some able-bodied event organizers and the condescending attitudes of some officials.

■ ACCOMPLISHMENTS (as a coach and organizer)

International Technical Delegate (ISMWSF and ISOD):

- IX Paralympiad, Barcelona 1992, Barcelona, Spain*
- World Championships and Games for the Disabled, Assen, The Netherlands, 1990
- World Stoke Mandeville Wheelchair Games, Aylesbury, England, 1990
- World Stoke Mandeville Wheelchair Games, Aylesbury, England, 1989
- Archery European Championships for the Disabled, Helsinki, Finland, 1989
- North American Open Wheelchair Archery Championships, Minneapolis, MA, USA, 1989

* (three years of preparation only; did not attend the actual event)

Coach:

- VIII Paralympic Games in Seoul, South Korea, 1988
- International Wheelchair Archery Championships, Hershey, PA, USA, 1987
- US National Archery Championships, Oxford, OH, USA, 1986
- VIII Pan American Games, Aguadilla, Puerto Rico, 1986
- US National Archery Championships, Oxford, OH, USA, 1985
- VII World Games for the Disabled, Aylesbury, England, 1984
- VII Pan American Wheelchair Games, Halifax, NS, 1982

Organizer:

- Member of the International Sports Technical Committee
- Technical Director for Canadian Wheelchair Sports Association from 1988 to 1992
- Chair of the International Archery Technical Committee from 1988 to 1992 for ISMWSF and ISOD
- Technical Director for the Federation of Canadian Archers from 1985 to 1988

BOCCIA

Boccia is a Paralympic sport based on the Italian game of boccia, which is played in parks worldwide. Paralympic boccia is a sport primarily developed for people with severe physical disabilities. The sport combines hand-eye co-ordination with wheelchair maneuverability skills and it is played by many athletes with cerebral palsy (CP). Athletes who use electric wheelchairs for mobility play boccia at the Paralympic and World

Championship level. Although boccia the sport of choice for athletes with severe cerebral palsy at national and international competitions such as the Paralympic Games, it is also a recreational and competitive game for people with many different disabilities. The official governing body of national and international competitions is the International Boccia Commission.

The ethos and spirit of boccia is similar to that of tennis and crowd participation is welcomed and encouraged. Spectators — including team members not on the court — are encouraged to remain quiet while players throw the ball. The purpose of boccia is to throw, kick, push, roll, or strike baseball-size leather balls of different colors towards a white target ball. A particularly notable feature of boccia is that it is a sport where men and women compete together in all events.

Paralympic boccia is a sport primarily developed for people with severe physical disabilities.

Boccia is played indoors on a smooth, flat, and non-slippery surface. This play area is a 12.5 metre by 6 metre rectangle, divided into several zones. The lines that mark the zones are 2 to 4 centimetres wide, and are made using tape (this tape is of a color easily distinguishable from the playing surface). These marking lines are then used to separate the playing area into three distinct zones.

The first zone is that from which the players operate. It consists of six 2.5 metre by 1 metre rectangles. The second zone is V-shaped, with its outer edges 3 metres wide and tapering down to a central width of 1.5 metres. If the target ball lands in this "V" shaped area, it is invalid. The remaining area makes up the third zone, which includes an X-shaped mark for the replaced target position; in the event of a tie, the target ball is placed here, and competitors attempt to place their ball as closely as possible to this point. Any ball that rolls outside of the outer marking lines of the playing area becomes a "dead ball."

Boccia is a simple game played by individuals, pairs or teams of three, and good strategy can compensate for lesser ability. Opponents take turns attempting to throw, kick, push, roll or strike their game-balls toward a white target ball. At the end of each round, points are awarded according to the proximity of the game-ball to the target ball. The player or team who maneuvers the balls closest to the target wins. Individual boccia is played with six balls per player for four rounds, while team boccia is played using two balls per player for six rounds. Because boccia balls are baseball-size leather balls, they are soft enough to be grasped by individuals with extreme fine motor difficulty, while still hard enough to roll. Players with very severe locomotor dysfunction have the option of using assistive devices such as ramps or chutes, usually made of plastic and aluminum pipe.

One of the world's top Boccia players, Paul Gauthier of Vancouver, accepts an award.

There are six divisions of play. Each division is played by competitors of both sexes. The divisions are for individual categories, and one each of pairs and teams. Players with limited disability may be assisted by one aide, who must remain seated at least 2 metres behind the playing box in a designated area. This aide may only come forward and assist if visibly requested by the player. These aides perform tasks such as adjusting or stabilising the playing chair or passing a ball to the player.

Players with very severe locomotor dysfunction in all four extremities of a cerebral or non-cerebral origin cannot propel the balls and are dependent on assistance or an electric wheelchair. An aide, who will remain in the player's box, but who must keep his or her back to court and eyes averted from play, may assist such players.

Pairs and teams are balanced according to the combined disability of their members. In pairs play, each player may be assisted by an aide as determined in rules relating to individual play. However, a player who uses an assistive device is not eligible to be a member of a team, though each team is allowed one aide who must abide by the rules laid down for individuals with limited disability.

■ Sport Highlight:

Canada is well represented in this sport. Paul Gauthier of Vancouver is one of the top boccia players in the world.

CROSS-COUNTRY SKIING

This sport got its start as a unique form of physical therapy for veterans. It has evolved into an enjoyable recreational pursuit for people of all ages and abilities. Inevitably, recreation gave birth to sport, and cross-country (or Nordic) skiing was introduced as an exhibition sport in the 1984 Paralympic Winter Games. It has been a Paralympic sport ever since.

Nordic skiing for athletes with disabilities is generally conducted over flat areas or on a combination of hilly and flat terrain. This is especially the case in sit-ski competitions for persons with paraplegia or other orthopedic impairments. Nordic ski trails vary significantly depending upon the disability of the athlete. Athletes who are deaf or hard of hearing, who have physical disabilities or who are blind or visually impaired may participate in the winter nordic ski competitions. Individuals and teams compete in timed individual male, female and team events. Rules are modified to allow equal competition amongst disability groups. The primary rule modifications that are made relate to equipment and the use of ski "companions." Sighted guides or companions are allowed for persons who are blind or have low vision. The guide may ski in front, behind or beside the blind skier to provide directional cueing in navigating the course and avoiding obstacles.

Most athletes in nordic skiing events use regulation cross-country skis and poles. Athletes are encouraged to utilize a three–layer system of clothing. Skiers who are blind or visually impaired wear a lightweight blind skier vest. Athletes with bilateral lower extremity amputation or lower extremity paralysis may use the nordic sit-ski sled to propel themselves across the course. (These athletes compete while seated on a chair equipped with two skis. Athletes' poles are shortened relative to their seated position.) Using the sled does require the athlete to have significant upper extremity and upper body muscular strength in order to pull their own body weight and the weight of the sled (an additional 10 to 40 pounds, depending on the type of sled). Pole lengths range from 50 to 135 centimeters, depending upon height and skill of the athlete.

Athletes at the Winter Paralympic games vie for medals using classical and freestyle skiing techniques.

Athletes at the Winter Paralympic games vie for medals using classical and freestyle skiing techniques and compete in both individual and team events. Events include races of 2.5 kilometres (sit skiers only), 5 kilometres, 10 kilometres, 15 kilometres (sit skiers only) and 20 kilometres.

ATHLETE PROFILE

bourgonje Colette

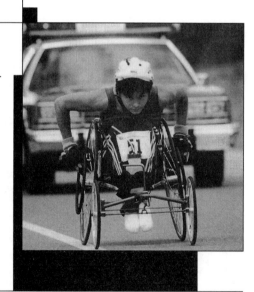

Key Events: Wheelchair athletics; Nordic cross-country skiing — 2.5 kilometres, 5 kilometres, 10 kilometres

Card: A

Classification: LW10

Birth date: 17/1/1962

Birthplace: Porcupine Plain, SK

Current Residence: Saskatoon, SK

PHOTO: *Colette Bourgonje competing in a wheelchair road race.*

■ Career Highlight

In 1996 Bourgonje was "A" carded, won two bronze medals in the Atlanta Paralympic Games and competed in the marathon

Colette Bourgonje is one of Canada's great wheelchair athletes and a veteran of two summer and two winter Paralympic Games. She has won numerous medals at the International Paralympic Committee (IPC) World Athletic Championships and the summer Paralympic Games, including three silver medals at the 1994 IPC World Athletic Championships and bronze medals in both the 100 metre and 200 metre wheelchair races at the 1996 Paralympics. At the 1998 Nagano Paralympics she won two silver medals and carried the Canadian flag at the closing ceremonies.

Throughout her life, Colette has broken down many barriers. As a youngster she played hockey with the boys, ignoring the jeers of her opponents. Later she was the first student in a wheelchair to graduate with a degree in physical education from the University of Saskatchewan. In 1996 she won the Individual Breakthrough Award presented by the Canadian Association for the Advancement of Women in Sport and Physical Activity. She is now actively involved in recruiting new athletes for the Saskatchewan Wheelchair Sport Association, and she visits schools to talk about the opportunities available to Paralympic athletes.

> *She was the first student in a wheelchair to graduate with a degree in physical education from the University of Alberta.*

Colette especially enjoys the sport of cross-country skiing. Getting outdoors and enjoying nature and the trails is motivating in itself, she says. She expresses her personal philosophy in the following words: "Work hard, train hard, and don't forget to thank the people who helped you along the way."

■ Competition History

1992 Winter Paralympic Games (Tignes, France)
- 2.5 kilometres — placed 6th
- 5 kilometres — placed 6th
- 10 kilometres — placed 6th

1994 Winter Paralympic Games (Lillehammer, Norway)
- 2.5 kilometres — placed 4th
- 5 kilometres — placed 4th
- 10 kilometres — placed 4th

1996 World Championships (Sunne, Sweden)
- 2.5 kilometres — placed 4th
- 5 kilometres — placed 4th
- 10 kilometres — placed 3rd

1997 Canadian Championships (North Battleford, SK, Canada)
- 2.5 kilometres — placed 1st

1998 Winter Paralympic Games (Nagano, Japan)
- 2.5 kilometres — placed 2nd
- 5 kilometres — placed 2nd

CYCLING

The speed and excitement inherent in all cycling competitions is very much a part of the cycling events in the Paralympic Games. Competitive cycling is relatively new for athletes with disabilities. Athletes with visual impairments were the first to compete in the early 1980s, followed by athletes with cerebral palsy and amputees, who began racing at the International Games for the Disabled (ISOD) in 1984. Until the 1992 Paralympics, the competitons for each of these different groups were held separately. Then, at the Barcelona Games, spectators witnessed intense competitions in both track and road races between athletes in all three disability groups. At the 1992 Barcelona Games, 149 cyclists (129 men and 20 women) from 19 delegations took part in the cycling competitions. In the time trial events for athletes with cerebral palsy, three new world cycling records were set. At the 1996 Summer Paralympic Games in Atlanta, cycling was one of the larger events staged — 125 competitors competed in 23 events.

Athletes with cerebral palsy, amputations and vision impairments all compete in Paralympic cycling events. Athletes with cerebral palsy compete using standard racing bikes and, in some classes, tricycles. Athletes who are blind or visually impaired compete on tandem bicycles with a sighted teammate, and they participate in the road race and the time trial events. Amputees and cyclists with permanent locomotor deficiencies compete in individual road race events using cycles specifically constructed for their needs. Cyclists who are deaf compete at the Summer World Games for the Deaf and

Jack MacDonnell and Kelly Thom racing in a blind tandem event.

athletes with mental disabilities compete in Special Olympics International Games.

Cycling road races can be held on any well paved road. When planning a road race it is very important to construct proper barriers that close the roads from motorized traffic and ensure the safety of the athletes and spectators. Track races are held on a velodrome — a steeply-banked, circular or oval track built specifically for cycle racing.

Cycling competitions are divided into individual and team events. Teams are comprised of three cyclists from a single nation. Athletes with vision impairments compete on tandem bicycles with a sighted teammate. The sighted rider in front is called the pilot or captain, and the visually impaired rider in the rear is called the stoker. Events include three divisions: mixed (one woman and one man), women (two women) and open (any combination of men and women). Athletes with cerebral palsy compete using standard racing cycles and, in some classifications, racing tricycles. Athletes with amputees and permanent locomotor disabilities compete using cycles specifically constructed for their needs. Prostheses are allowed and some athletes use arm-driven bicycles. Athletes who are deaf compete using racing bicycles in road racing and track events. Track cycles have no brakes and only one gear, which is sized according to the riding style of the athlete and the event. Road bikes vary widely between events and are specialized in nature, often incorporating as many as 27 gears. Helmets are required in all competitions and must be either ANSI or Snell approved. During competition, cycling shorts, jerseys and shoes with a cleat/pedal system must be worn.

People with visual impairments use tandem bicycles, which they ride with a guide.

■ Sport Highlight:

Top Canadian cyclists include amputee Patrice Bonneau of Laval, Quebec; CP athlete Gary Longhi of Montreal, Quebec; and blind rider Julie Cournoyer of Sherbrooke, Quebec. All three athletes received medals at the 1996 Paralympics.

EQUESTRIAN

B alance, rhythm, precision … these are the qualities that define equestrian competition. In the Summer Paralympics, equestrian events are open to athletes with cerebral palsy, physical disabilities, visual impairments, blindness or mental disabilites. Spectators at witness competitors in the dressage event who demonstrate harmony with their horse, and perform world-class routines with high levels of balance, rhythm, energy and precision.

Horseback riding is well recognized for its ability to improve posture, lower extremity strength, balance, joint mobility and muscle control. Therapeutic programs are often referred to as "hippotherapy" or physical therapy using the horse as a therapy tool to address the movement disorders associated with various neurological and neuromuscular disorders (i.e. cerebral palsy, cerebral vascular accidents or stroke, traumatic brain injury, multiple sclerosis). Hippotherapy was introduced in Europe following the outbreak of poliomyelitis after World War II. Equestrian events were included within the Paralympic Games as demonstration events in 1976 but it was not until 1996 that they became competitive events.

The horse and rider who come together as a team are invariably at the top of the competition.

Persons with spinal injuries, amputations, cerebral palsy, vision impairments and les autres conditions are eligible to participate in this Paralympic sport. Equestrian events are the only events in which persons with visual impairments may compete with persons with orthopedic impairment. Regulation indoor or fenced outdoor arenas are used for competition. Competitive show rings are a minimum of 200 meters by 200 meters. Dressage rings are 20 meters by 40 meters. A mounting area with a ramp and block are also provided.

Paralympic athletes are judged on showmanship or the ability to maneuver, direct and control the horse through a variety of tasks. Both the rider and horse are evaluated throughout the competition. Athletes compete in dressage in seven medal events:

- Individual Championships (4 classes)
- National Team Championships
- Individual Championship Kur (trot)
- Individual Championship Kur (canter)

At the Paralympic Games, riders compete on borrowed horses, thereby eliminating the issues of transportation cost and the horses' adjustment to changing climates. Riders typically wear long breeches to protect their legs from irritation from the saddle. Fleece saddle covers are often recommended for athletes diagnosed with paraplegia to prevent pressure sores. Boots are typically worn to maintain the feet in the stirrups. Hard shoes with heels, boots, or tennis shoes with heels are required for competition unless medical reasons prevent the athlete from wearing them. Riding helmets or head protective gear are required. Western or English saddles may be selected.

Disability-specific equipment is also commonly used. A Humes rein is used by persons with poor hand control. The reins are secured together and two oval loops are added at an equal distance from the bit. The rider inserts his or her hands into the loops allowing them to control the horse with their wrist or arm. The Devonshire boot — actually a boot-like device — can be used to replace the stirrup and assists individuals with foot or ankle deformities and/or weakness. The Devonshire boot is utilized to prevent the rider's feet from slipping out of the stirrup. The Peacock stirrup is designed for safety with one side of the stirrup made of iron and the opposite side made of "breakaway" material such as rubber or elastic. In the case of a fall or significant pressure, the breakaway side releases to prevent the rider from getting his or her foot caught in the stirrup. Saddles with supportive back rests have been designed for persons with quadriplegia. However, even with this device, persons with quadripalegia will require assistance from an able-bodied assistant. Bucket-like seats can also be constructed to assist the person with bilateral lower-extremity amputations with minimal residual limbs. In competition no device is allowed that would affix the rider to the horse. An access ramp constructed according to the Paralympic code (one inch elevation to twelve inches in distance) is designed so that the person with mobility impairment can wheel or walk up the ramp to saddle the horse. For ease in saddling the horse, ramps should have a resting or saddling platform of five feet by five feet.

Rules allow for the use of side walkers or "ground assistants." Walkers are not allowed to walk in front of the horse nor are they allowed to coach the athlete during competition. Sight-impaired riders may either use beepers or callers to provide directional cues in the ring. Callers are limited in number to nine and are given specific protocol for positioning in the ring. Riders with a hearing impairment may have an assistant to interpret the judge's directions to the rider.

In dressage competition, riders perform individually and they must ride a pattern which includes various changes in pace and direction. At the Paralympics, all riders are grouped according to their functional profiles and judged on their ability to control and maneuver the horses. Functional profiles are used at Regional, World and Paralympic Competitions. Athletes are classified according to their ability to control and maneuver the horse in the following events: walk; walk and trot; more advanced walk and trot; walk, trot and canter; or more advanced walk, trot and canter. Physical categorisation of an athlete's degee of disability takes into account the degree to which a rider: is ambulatory or wheelchair-bound with subsequent ability for sitting balance; has reduced function of muscle strength and mobility and/or spasticity in all limbs; displays asymmetry and is prone to extreme fatigue; extent and multiplicity of amputation; blindness or sight-impairment; cerebral-palsic or brain injured, affecting physical ability; multiplegic, athetoid or ataxic; affected by spinal injuries or polio. In the event of borderline classification on the ground, the rider will be tested on horseback by the independent Doctor and Sports Technician/ Technical Delegate, who will make the final decision.

The Canadian Therapeutic Riding Association (CanTRA) is a large organization with established branches from coast to coast. For the most part, CanTRA administers competitive equestrian events for people with disabilities in Canada.

■ SPORT HIGHLIGHT

Successful athletes include two-time World Dressage medallist Maria Simpson of Woodbridge, Ontario, and Burnaby, British Columbia's Gregg Honour.

GOALBALL

G oalball was invented in 1946 by an Austrian athlete, Hanz Lorencezen, and the German athlete Sett Reindle. The game was used for sport and as a rehabilitation activity for post-World War II veterans who were blind. The game of goalball developed over the years. In 1980 it gained international acceptance and became a Paralympic sport.

Goalball is one of the few sports that originate from within the disability community. The adaptations used in the sport enable players — with or without sight — to compete on an equal basis. Players must wear eyeshades to ensure that each player has an equal lack of vision. One of the essential

Goalball is a cross between soccer and team handball.

Blind athletes playing goalball.

components of the game is the players' ability to hear the large medicine ball, which contains a bell. To ensure audibility of the ball, thus allowing players to compete, spectators must remain in perfect silence. Only when a point is scored or the referee holds up play can the audience show its appreciation.

Goalball is a cross between soccer and team handball. The object of the game is simply to roll the ball on the floor in a bowling motion and have the ball completely cross over the opposing team's goal line, thereby scoring a point. A regular goalball game is 14 minutes long, consisting of two seven-minute halves with a three-minute half time so that the teams can switch ends. There are teams in both men's and women's divisions.

Canada has developed a strong goalball program, especially since 1980. A national goalball championship occurs annually, and Canada has hosted several international tournaments.

■ Sport Highlight

Canada has consistently provided highly ranked national teams in this disability specific sport. In 1994 the national team earned fifth place at the World Championship and won the silver medal at the Porto International Cup.

JUDO

Judo is a competitive sport (also called a martial art) in which people with visual impairment can fully participate without major accommodations. Judo has been included in the Paralympic program since the Seoul Games in 1988. Four years later, at the Barcelona 1992 Games, 53 athletes representing 16 countries took part in the judo competition.

In judo, two players compete in matches that may last from two to five minutes, each trying to win by throwing, pinning, choking, or applying an arm bar to the opponent.

The only signs that the judo competitions at the Paralympic Games are different from other top level judo events are the varied textures on the mats indicating competition area and zones. Athletes who are blind or have a visual impairment compete for the medals, and the competition rules follow those of the International Judo Federation. The same high calibre of competition as in all other international judo events is immediately evident at the Paralympics.

Judo is growing in popularity among females, who competed at the demonstration sport level in the 1996 Atlanta Paralympics.

In the Paralympic Games, athletes who are classified as having visual impairment (classes B1, B2, and B3 in a combined open classification) are eligible to participate in judo competitions. Both male and female athletes are classified for competitions on the basis of their weight (seven separate weight classes for each gender). Until the Barcelona Paralympic in 1992, only male blind athletes were eligible to compete in this event, but judo is growing in popularity among females, who competed at the demonstration sport level in the 1996 Atlanta Paralympic.

Judo is played indoors. Athletes (*judokas*) wear a uniform called the Judogi and compete on a tatami — the rectangular competition-area mat made of pressed foam rubber — as in all international judo championships. The playing surface is on a raised platform which is divided into two sections. There is a 10 metre by 10 metre mat on which the competitors struggle, as well as a 1-metre wide official "danger strip" around the edge of the playing zone — a heated surface to warn athletes that they are getting close to falling off the platform. The most important rule difference between Paralympic and Olympic judo is the initial touch before the referee's command to start in Paralympic competitions. In other words, the Paralympic referee claps both athletes' shoulders to signal them to prepare for competition. There is no disability-specific equipment.

In a judo competition, two opponents from the same weight category compete in a match that lasts up to five minutes or as quickly as the time it takes to score a full point called an *Ippon*, which is won by throwing the opponent straight on his or her back or pinning the opponent down for 25 seconds. Other scoring terms in judo that can equal an *Ippon* (full point) or that can be used to determine a winner in case competitors don't score a full point include:

Waza-ari: a half point scored by throwing opponent partially on his/her back or pinning down for 20 seconds (two *waza-aris* equal one full point);

Yuko: equal to a quarter point, but cannot add up to an Ippon or end a match. Is scored by throwing an opponent on his or her side or thigh or pinning down for 15 seconds;

Koka: equal to an eighth of a point, but cannot add up to an Ippon or end a match. Is scored by throwing opponent on buttocks or pinning down for 10 seconds.

A *Waza-ari* will always place higher than all *Yuko*'s combined, and a *Yuko* will always place higher than all *Koka's* combined.

Burnaby, BC's Pierre Morton is one of the top Paralympic competitors in the world.

LAWN BOWLING

F ocus, orientation and discipline: Lawn bowling is one of the oldest sports played today and is most popular in Britain and the Commonwealth countries. It dates back to at least the 14th century. The most prestigious lawn bowling competitions for people with disabilities occur at the International Stoke Mandeville Games, the National Wheelchair Championships (British Wheelchair Sports Foundation) and the Paralympic Games.

Lawn bowling continues to be one of the most popular recreational and competitive sports for people with disabilities in Canada. In 1992 lawn bowling became a Paralympic sport.

Lawn bowling is unique in that it can be played by both men and women at any age and with a variety of disabilities. This sport is open to wheelchair athletes, cerebral palsy athletes, athletes with physical disabilities and visually impaired or blind athletes. Individuals with disabilities can and do play at the club and international level, often with and against able-bodied bowlers.

The athletes at the Paralympic Games are selected to represent their country after taking part in national championships. At the Paralympics, competitions are organized according to functional classes so that the players compete against others of equal playing abilities. The Paralympic program includes men's, women's, mixed singles, pairs, triples and fours events. These competitions are open to individuals with physical disabilities, wheelchair athletes, athletes with cerebral palsy, and blind and visually impaired athletes. Athletes are categorised according to their disability. As in all international competitions, the World Bowls Board rules govern the competitions; however, some rules have been amended so as to accommodate bowlers with a disability. The playing area is called a rink and is approximately 120 feet by 14 feet. Most rinks are made of grass and are located outside. Often, many rinks are lined up side by side, forming a square level area called a green. The green is surrounded by a ditch that is between 8 and 15 inches wide and 2 to 8 inches deep.

Lawn bowling for the visually impaired was a featured sport at the 1994 Commonwealth Games.

The rules of lawn bowling are similar to those in boccia. A small white target ball, called a jack, is placed into play. Athletes then take turns rolling larger wooden balls, called bowls, towards the target ball, attempting to get as close to it as possible. Athletes may also decide to roll balls to areas of the rink in anticipation that the target ball may end up in that area after it is struck by other bowls. Each athlete is allowed four bowls, which are rolled from a matted area. There are no changes in rules for lawn bowling for athletes with disabilities. Blind athletes play by the same rules but use assistants during competition. Canes and chairs are allowed but no chutes or ramps are permitted for disabled athletes during formal competition.

Little equipment is needed for this sport — simply a jack, four bowls per player and a mat (about 24 inches by 14 inches) from which to throw. The jack should be white and $2^1/_3$ inches in diameter. The bowls are usually wood or rubber and painted brown or black. Bowls are about $5^1/_8$ inches in diameter and have a mark that identifies the player. The weight of the bowl should not exceed three pounds, eight ounces.

British Columbia is the central location for this sport in Canada, particularly after lawn bowling for the visually impaired was a featured sport at the 1994 Commonwealth Games in Victoria, British Columbia.

■ SPORT HIGHLIGHT

Ed McMillan of the Courtenay Lawn Bowling Club in Courtenay, BC is the most successful visually impaired lawn bowler in Canada, finishing in second place at the 1995 World Championship in the singles division.

POWERLIFTING

Although it is one of the most controversial sports for people with disabilities because it is perceived to be dangerous, powerlifting in one form or another has been around since the very first Paralympic Games in 1960.

Prior to 1994 there were several different versions of powerlifting for athletes with disabilities — for example, each category of physical disability had its own variation of the bench-press lift. In 1994, under the auspices of the International Paralympic Committee (IPC), each international disability organization gave up control of its own version of the sport in favour of a single, multi-disability method of lifting.

Weightlifting at the 1985 Canadian Games.

Although there were many opponents to this significant change, powerlifting for athletes with mobility impairments is today one of the most popular Paralympic sports. Any athlete who can fully extend his or her upper limbs can compete in the sport — amputees compete against athletes who are paraplegics or who've had polio, as well as athletes with cerebral palsy.

The popularity of this sport amongst Canadian athletes with a disability has waxed and waned over the years. The present lack of a Canada Games for the Physically Disabled means that most lifters are not able to compete in games that also feature other sports. As well, the structure of disability sport within Canada — which is increasingly a sport-specific structure, not a disability-specific model — has left powerlifting behind. No single disability or sport organization has taken charge of the sport. Because the Canadian Powerlifting Union (CPU) is a small organization with no federal funding or staff, powerlifters with a disability are much worse off under the sport-specific model and the sport has suffered immensely in recent years. This can be seen particularly at the competitive level. Whereas in 1985 it would not have been uncommon to see 15 or 20 lifters at the Canada Games for the Physically Disabled (the games were still taking place then), in 1996 Canada sent three lifters to the Atlanta Paralympic Games. There are no national powerlifting championships for lifters with a disability.

Powerlifting for athletes with mobility impairments is one of the most popular Paralympic sports.

For several years — from 1992 to 1995 — lifters did have the opportunity to compete in the non-disabled bench-press championships sanctioned by the CPU. However, in 1995 the CPU and its international body — the International Powerlifting Federation (IPF) — chose to ban all amputees and lifters who wore prostheses. Sadly, this worldwide ban is still in effect and all attempts to amend this rule have been uniformly quashed. The lack of acceptance for powerlifting within the overall sport community certainly does not help the cause of powerlifters with disabilities. While powerlifting in the non-disabled community is not an Olympic event, the sport *is* a Paralympic-level event. This is a factor that the IPF should have take into consideration before enforcing a rule that has resulted in the banning of a significant number of athletes from the sport.

Powerlifting is incredibly popular at the international level, but the burden of organizing Canada's lifters seems to be too much for the national sport structure to bear. Ironically, in the last few years the CPU has cleaned up its act, and lifters on banned substances are no longer allowed to compete. Yet the sport has not been rewarded for its affirmative action; instead, it has been cut off from all federal funding. The result is that the sport of powerlifting remains in logistical limbo for Canadian athletes with a disability.

Powerlifting is also a non-Paralmpic sport for athletes with a visual impairment, and several Canadian powerlifting records are held by blind athletes.

■ SPORT HIGHLIGHTS

Over 220 lifters competed at the first combined World Powerlifting Championship for the Disabled in 1994. Canada's top lifters include Toronto's Andrew Wrzeszcz in the 100 kilogram-plus class (he lifts 215-220 kg.) and Newfoundland's Ken Doyle in the 67.5 kilogram class (see profile).

ATHLETE PROFILE

lee ann *dalling*

Key Event: Powerlifting (Bench Press)

Card: uncarded

Classification: 48 kilogram bodyweight

Current Residence: New Glasgow, NS

■ Career Highlight

Silver medal at the International Powerlifting Federation's (IPF) Bench Press World Championship in Denmark, November 1996

Lee Ann Dalling is one of the few athletes with a disability in Canada who has rarely participated in "disabled" events. She competes in "able-bodied" events and has been very successful. Her November 1996 silver medal at the International Powerlifting Federation's Bench Press World Championship confirmed that Lee Ann Dalling is one of the world's top bench pressers. She may soon be the first person with a disability to become a powerlifting world champion.

Lee Ann Dalling lives in New Glasgow, Nova Scotia. Her first meet was in December 1993, at the Eastern Canada Powerlifting Championships in Antigonish, Nova Scotia. She won the 48-kilogram class with a lift of 57.5 kilograms, to break the Nova Scotia and Atlantic Region records. This qualified her to compete at the Bench Nationals in May 1994.

In April 1994, Lee Ann won the Best Lifter award at a qualifier event just days after being released from hospital with the flu. In May she went on to win the Canadian Champion title at the Nationals, which qualified her to go to Finland for the Bench Press Worlds. She placed a very respectable sixth at the Worlds. In 1995 she competed in the Bench Nationals in Chilliwack, British Columbia, where she was again the champion, benching 52.5 in the 44-kilogram class. In 1996 she won the silver medal in the bench press at the World Championship.

Lee Ann is the first woman with a disability to win the Canadian title against able-bodied athletes.

Lee Ann is the first woman with a disability to win the Canadian title against able-bodied athletes and may be the first in her weight class to qualify and compete in a world event. She was named "Female Athlete of the Month" for December 1995 by Sport

Nova Scotia, and her accomplishments were discussed in the Nova Scotia legislature. She has also been approached by both the Canadian Broadcasting Corporation (CBC) and The Sports Network (TSN) for interviews and was featured in an issue of *Musclemag International*.

Lee Ann trains three to four times a week, for approximately two hours per day. She competes in both the 44 kilogram and 48 kilogram weight classes, and actually lifted in the Women's Bench World Championship on the one-year anniversary of her very first powerlifting contest. "I've always known I was stronger than the average person, mainly because I've walked with crutches and braces since I was three," she says. "This has given me tremendous upper body strength. I hate to lose at anything, but a [disabled only] world title is not as important as competing in able-bodied classes in an effort to remove the attitudinal barriers and stereotypes that exist with regard to persons with disabilities."

ATHLETE PROFILE

ken doyle

Key Event: Powerlifting

Card: uncarded

Classification: 67.5 kilogram bodyweight

Birthdate: 19/03/1977

Birthplace: Toronto, ON

Current Residence: St. John's, NF

Career Highlight

Set the record for the Canadian Powerlifting Union (CPU) 67.5 kilogram class (in Junior category) in 1992

In 1992, at the age of seventeen, Ken Doyle broke into the world of powerlifting for athletes with a disability, smashing Canadian records as he went. While that might have been sufficient accomplishment for most athletes with a disability, Ken had (and took) the opportunity to concentrate on non-disabled powerlifting as well. In that same year, Ken set a non-disabled bench-press record at the Eastern Regional Championships in the Junior category. His press of 160 kilograms in the 67.5 kilogram class still stands today.

Shortly after setting this new Canadian mark, Ken headed off to Finland to compete in the non-disabled Bench Press World Championships. Little did Ken know that the liberal attitudes of Canadians toward athletes with a disability had yet to reach the powerlifting elite in other nations.

Ken uses a set of leg braces and a pair of forearm crutches in order to give him mobility;

he does not use a wheelchair. So when Ken travelled all the way to the lifting platform at the IPF Bench Press World Championship, he was expecting to do well. The audience of 3000 spectators were full of anticipation at the opportunity to see this young Canadian lifter in action. On his first attempt, however, Ken was stopped as he was about to make his way to the elevated lifting platform. The judges told Ken that leg braces were not allowed in IPF-sanctioned bench-press meets and he had three minutes to remove them or miss his first attempt. It takes Ken at least 10 minutes to remove his leg braces; as a result, he missed his opening lift.

On the second lift attempt he encountered further difficulties. Since Ken cannot move without his leg braces and crutch combination, the Canadian coach assisted Ken to the lifting platform. The judges again stopped Ken, saying that coaches were not permitted to assist lifters onto the lifting platform. The time allotted for the second attempt ran out.

On his third and final attempt, in full view of his fellow lifters and 3000 spectators, Ken was made to crawl from the warm-up area to the lifting platform. Despite this demeaning and inhumane act on the part of the officials, Ken salvaged his opening lift weight of 157.5 kilograms.

Ken Doyle had travelled thousands of miles to be treated in a fashion that no Olympic athlete should and would submit to.

The audience was outraged at this treatment of a competitive lifter, and the Canadian team manager quickly lodged a complaint. Ken Doyle had travelled thousands of miles to be treated in a fashion that no Olympic athlete should and would submit to.

Later, the officials stated that Ken Doyle's treatment was not their fault — they were simply following the written rules for the sport. The officials also stated that someone from the Canadian team should have enforced the rules, thereby preventing the controversy from arising in the first place.

Back in Canada the shameful treatment of Ken Doyle went unnoticed. The Canadian Amputee Sports Association did nothing. The CPU was outvoted 42 to 1 at the next IPF assembly when the Canadian group suggested amending the rules to allow lifters with mobility impairments to use their prosthetic limbs or leg braces. To this day, amputees who use prosthetic legs and lifters with mobility impairments are banned from competing in IPF-sanctioned events. Ken Doyle still competes — in the disabled section of powerlifting events.

SAILING

When Margaret Thatcher gave Rick Hansen a British-made Sunbird sailboat in honour of his Man in Motion tour in 1986, she did not know that her gift would open up the world of sailing to hundreds of people with severe disabilities across Canada. In 1989 Rick Hansen asked Sam Sullivan, a quadriplegic, to use the specially adapted boat to start a sailing program for people with disabilities. This led to the birth of the

Sip-and-puff controls in action on the Martin 16 sailboat.

Disabled Sailing Association of British Columbia (DSA–BC). Within a few short years, DSA–BC had a total of 16 Sunbird sailboats distributed among three chapters located in British Columbia (in Vancouver, Victoria and Kelowna).

Since its start in 1989, the DSA–BC has made steady progress on two fronts: providing increasing numbers of disabled individuals with solo and accompanied sailing experiences; and equipping boats to accommodate individuals with progressively greater levels of disability. A breakthrough in these objectives came in 1993 when "sip-and-puff" controls were added to a Sunbird sailboat, permitting solo sailing by "high quads" (individuals with no physical ability below the neck). Sip-and-puff sailing involves the same principles of operating a sip-and-puff wheelchair. Using a specially designed mouthpiece, the sailor bites on a rubber bubble tip to change the controls from sails to rudder and vice versa. Blowing through the straw will draw the rudder to port, or let the sails out (depending on which control the sailor is operating at the time); sucking through the straw will draw the rudder to starboard, or pull the sails in. When the sailor stops sipping or puffing, the boat will maintain its position and course.

Although modification of the Sunbird to include sip-and-puff control and necessary safety features proved to be a critical juncture in the development of the sport — the challenging objective of preparing a boat so that a high quad could sail had been achieved — the boat was still less than ideal in terms of sailing capability. Recognizing this, the DSA–BC, in conjunction with other local organizations, took on the challenge of creating an all-new boat design that would not only accommodate the requirements of sailors with various disabilities, but would also be a high performance sailboat with potential for future "class" recognition.

Among those who rallied in support of upgrading technology for high-quad sailing and developing a new sailboat were the Neil Squire Foundation, the Science Council of British Columbia, Martin Yachts Ltd., Robert B. Harris Ltd., the Marine Trades

Association and the Royal Bank. The result — the Martin 16 — was unveiled at the Royal Vancouver Yacht Club on July 26, 1995.

Today, the DSA-BC is seeking financial partners to assist with the acquisition of at least three new M16s for its fleet. The association is also working with programs in the Canadian cities of Calgary, Toronto, Ottawa, Halifax, Moncton, Sarnia and Montreal, and in the states of Washington and Oregon in the United States. Athletes with disabilities sail and compete under the umbrella of the Canadian Yachting Association.

Internationally, sailing was introduced as a demonstration sport at the 1996 Atlanta Paralympic Games. Sailing is a recommended sport for persons of many disability groups. Individuals who are hard of hearing or deaf, blind or visually impaired, spinal cord injured, amputee, as well as those with other orthopedic and neuromuscular disorders, are encouraged to engage in sailing as a recreational sport. Individuals who are blind may compete in the World Blind Sailing Championship. These were held in 1992, 1994 and 1997. The classification standards for Sailing in the Paralympic Games were designed for crews that includes athletes with all types of disabilities, with classification based on hearing, vision, hand function, maneuverability, and stability. From the observation of top sailors, it has been possible to identify the degree to which different functional limitations affect the ability to undertake the functions of sailing. Therefore the loss of hearing or the use of a foot are regarded as less functionally disabling in sailing than they might be in other sports. Generally, if a sailor has several functional limitations, it is the one which scores the least points which counts.

Modification of the Sunbird to include sip-and-puff controls and necessary safety features proved to be a critical juncture in the development of the sport.

It is further recognised that certain combinations of functions are more functionally disabling than others. For example, someone with poor stability and poor hand function is given less points than someone with only one of these limitations. However, someone with poor hearing and without a foot is not regarded as doubly disabled in this context. Each crew of three sailors is allowed a maximum of 12 points. If somebody with a low disability (7 points) wishes to participate he or she may only sail with two people with more severe disabilities (for example somebody with 1 and another with 2 points). It is theoretically possible to have three very disabled people sailing together, for example each with one point, but this crew would not be given any sporting advantage over a less disabled crew.

There are primarily two types of racing: handicapped and one-design. In a one-design race (i.e. a Paralympic regatta), all boats are constructed using the same design specifications, and the first boat crossing the finish line wins the race. In the handicapped design race, boats of various ratings compete against the clock and the fastest corrected time wins.

In the Paralympic Games there are two basic types of courses: the long distance and the closed-course. The closed-course is also referred to as "round the buoys" racing. Courses are designed with markers or buoys that the competitors must maneuver around or pass on a specified side. This racing method lasts anywhere from 15 minutes to 4 hours in length. Multiple races are held in a regatta.

Sailboat racing is governed by the International Yacht Racing Rules. Athletes are expected to enforce the rules themselves. The basic principle is that the first boat crossing the finish line wins. In a regatta, the low-point rule system is most commonly utilized.

One point is scored for first place, two points are awarded for second place, three points are earned for third place, etc. Upon completion of all races the sum of all race finishes will be added and the lowest points win.

Sailors competing in the World Blind Sailing Championships are allowed to maintain a crew of four, two visually impaired and two sighted sailors. A person who is visually impaired is the helmsman steer and the blind crew person can take any other function on the boat. The sighted crew members are not allowed to touch the tiller, with the exception of emergency situations. The sighted skipper can provide verbal cueing to the visually impaired helmsperson and blind crew person. The sighted skipper is also allowed to trim the backstay. The second sighted crew person can take on any other function on the boat, but is not allowed to steer.

Foam-rubber seat cushions, or Rohos, are often recommended for the comfort of persons with mobility impairment. Extra hand holds are recommended for the person diagnosed with paraplegia to compensate for balance issues that occur on a boat that would otherwise not be an issue on land. Back supports are recommended to add torso support and stability for athletes with high level thoracic injuries. Athletes with physical disabilities may require transfer aids such as a sliding board (a board between the wheelchair and the boat that allows the person to "slide" onto the boat with minimal assistance), a transfer box (similar to the sliding board but his device allows the person to transfer onto the box on shore and "slide" onto the boat from an attached sliding board, this device also provides a back rest for those requiring additional trunk support), or a hoyer lift sling or webbing loop (devices that secure around the torso and hips of the athlete with disability and through a hydraulic or pump system lower the person into the boat). The hoyer or sling systems require a hoist be installed on a stable dock.

■ SPORT HIGHLIGHTS

Since its inception, the DSA-BC program has provided children and adults with over 5000 sailing experiences and recruited over 400 volunteers. In competition, Team Canada gave a gold medal performance at the 1996 Paralympics in Atlanta.

SHOOTING

Paralympic shooting competitions include rifle (smallbore and air rifle) and pistol events defined by the type of shooting position (prone, kneeling and standing). The Paralympic program includes men's, women's and mixed events.

Athletes shoot at non-reflective targets within nine concentric circles. The scoring ranges from one to 10, with the innermost ring worth 10 points. All events are completed in an uninterrupted series of 10 shots. No lens, lens systems or telescopic sights are permitted. Corrective lenses may be worn by the shooter.

Glenn Mariash of the Manitoba shoots at a target.

All competitors are classified as SH1 or SH2, in one of three or four categories:

Class SH1

SH1A: Standing or sitting competitors without backrest and with normal balance;

SH1B: Sitting competitors with a low backrest (one third of the back) and good balance;

SH1C: Sitting competitors with a backrest of 10 centimetres below the armpits and fair balance. An angle of 20 degrees is allowed; SH1D: Sitting competitors with a backrest of 10 centimetres below the armpits and poor or no balance. An angle of 30 degrees is allowed.

Class SH2

SH2A: Shooters who require a shooting stand to support the rifle, with a backrest and normal balance;

SH2B: Shooters who require a shooting stand to support the rifle, with a low backrest (one third of the back) and good balance;

SH2C: Shooters who require a shooting stand to support the rifle, with a backrest of 10 centimetres below the armpits and fair to poor balance. An angle of 20 degrees is allowed.

◾ SPORT HIGHLIGHT

Among Canadians, top athletes include Laszlo Decsi, who was the gold medal winner in the Free Pistol Event at the 1992 Paralympics (see profile).

laszlo decsi

Key Event: Shooting

Card: A

Classification: SH1

Birthdate: 22/12/1934

Birthplace: Budapest, Hungary

Current Residence: Tweed, ON

■ CAREER HIGHLIGHTS

Gold medal winner, Barcelona Paralympics, 1992; Canadian Paralympic team member since 1980

In 1979 a rumour was circulating about an amputee who had competed at the shooting nationals and placed among the top three competitors in his event. Canadian Amputee Sports Association (CASA) president John Gibson called up the competitor, Laszlo Decsi, to discover the truth — and sure enough, it turned out that Laszlo was an above-knee amputee. He was promptly inducted onto the amputee national team, despite the fact that he had never competed against fellow amputees. Laszlo went on to represent Canada at the 1980 Paralympics in Holland, winning a silver medal in the air pistol category. Interestingly, one of his earliest disappointments was at the medal presentation ceremony for this event. "No Canadians showed up!" he remembers.

Laszlo placed among the top five Canadian competitors in the free pistol, centre fire, rapid fire and air pistol disciplines.

Laszlo Decsi's history as a marksman is closely related to his history as an amputee. He lost his leg in 1972 and the following year took up the sport of shooting; by 1975 Laszlo was the first amputee member of the Canadian National shooting team. Laszlo placed among the top five Canadian competitors in the free pistol, centre fire, rapid fire and air pistol disciplines from 1975 to 1986. At the 1976 Olympic trials he placed third, narrowly missing a spot on the Canadian Olympic Team.

Despite these achievements, Laszlo's claim to fame as one of Canada's top marksmen was not without controversy. In 1983, Canada's national team manager, Bill Hare, lodged a complaint against Laszlo with the International Shooting Union (ISU), saying that Laszlo's prosthetic limb should be regarded as an artificial support. It took almost 18 months — during which photos and verbal descriptions were sent to the ISU — before the matter was resolved. Finally, the technical director with the ISU determined the prosthesis was not an artificial support, enabling Laszlo (and any other amputee shooter) to continue representing his country at international events.

Today, at age 63, Laszlo Decsi finds that his greatest reward comes from simply competing, regardless of whether he is participating in a non-disabled Canadian national shooting event or representing Canada at the Paralympics. He regards his gold medal win at the 1992 Barcelona Paralympics, which was followed by a reception in Ottawa that honoured Paralympic and Olympic athletes equally, as the highlight of his career.

SLEDGE HOCKEY

Sledge hockey was initially developed by former members of the Swedish national hockey team following an airplane crash in which several team members became paraplegics. The sport came to Canada in 1980 when a team was founded in Medicine Hat, Alberta. Today, Sledge Hockey is a Paralympic sport. Team Sweden has dominated the sport for many years.

Athletes with locomotor disabilities and who comply with the International Paralympic Committee (IPC) classifications for sitting winter sports are eligible to compete. Each player must have a permanent disability that prevents the athlete from playing regular ice hockey. Determination of minimum disability and appropriate classification is made by authorized winter sport classifiers. A maximum of 12 players, including goalies, constitute a team. To ensure the maximum participation of athletes with physical disabilities, a classification system has been developed for three groups of players. Each player has a different point value on the ice (rated from one to three, depending on functional disability). The point value for a team on the ice, including the goalie, may not exceed 15 points.

The playing area is an ice rink of standard size (100 feet wide by 200 feet long) with standard-size goals. The same markings, circles and boundary lines as those used in regulation hockey exist. The rink, team benches and penalty boxes must have plexiglass shields and ideally there should be level access to the ice surface, allowing the athletes to enter and exit the ice without assistance or lifting by support staff or coaches. The rink and penalty-box areas should be ice-covered or rubber-matted to help avoid damage to the players' sleds.

Rules are modified using the International Ice Federation hockey rules for the able-bodied. Most rule modifications involve the use of the athlete's sled or stick. Sledge hockey equipment includes sledges, sticks, goalkeeper's equipment and protective equipment. Sledges can

A game of sledge hockey.

measure from ice to bottom of frame at 8.5 to 9.5 cm. Frames cannot exceed $^1/_3$ the length of the sledge. Seat cushions cannot be more than 10 cm in height. The sledge can have a back rest, but the back cannot protrude laterally beyond armpits or have rounded edges and corners. Straps can be used to secure the player's body to the sledge. A puck must be able to roll on edge under the sledge.

The stick cannot be more than 75 cm in length. The depth of teeth must be equal to or less than 4 mm. Pick-ends must be fixed to the lower or butt end of stick and cannot end in a single, sharp point. The pick-end must have 6 teeth per stick. Pick ends can be made of any material but cannot exceed the width of stick nor be longer than 10.2 cm. The blade cannot be more than 5 cm in height or 25 cm in length. Edges on sticks must be rounded to 3 mm corners. Grooves in the blade-end cannot be more than 1.27 cm ($^1/_2$ inch).

Each player must have a permanent disability that prevents the athlete from playing regular ice hockey.

The goalkeeper's sticks cannot be more than 35 cm in length and 11 cm in height. Goalkeepers can wear mitts and other protective gear. Picks on gear cannot be more than 44 mm protuberances and teeth cannot exceed 4 mm. It is recommended that all players wear protective gear as defined by the hockey rules for able-bodied ice-hockey players.

Seated on a "sledge" equipped with two skate blades fixed to the bottom, players grip miniature hockey sticks in both hands. The sledges, which allow the puck to pass underneath, replace skates, and the players use sticks with a spike-end and a blade-end. With a quick flip of the wrist, the players are able to propel themselves using the spikes and then play the puck using the blade-end of the sticks. A player may use two sticks with blades in order to facilitate stick handling and ambidextrous shooting. If a puck is stuck or unplayable under player's sledge, the referee stops play and there is a face off. Goalkeepers cannot lay down the sides of the sledge to stop a shot. If they do, this action results in a penalty shot.

Sledge hockey is a fast-paced game and requires frequent player changes. A complete game is comprised of three 15-minute stop-time periods. Overtime consists of one 10-minute period. If there is still a tie after overtime, the winner is determined by a shoot-out.

The Canadian national sledge hockey team has acquitted itself well in Paralympic and international championship tournaments (recently placing third behind Sweden and Norway at the World Championships). But uneven provincial development hampers the growth of the sport. In British Columbia, an average turnout at a practice might be a mere 15 players, some of whom are able-bodied players. In other provinces, such as Alberta and Ontario, the sport is more popular and a number of teams play against each other.

◼ SPORT HIGHLIGHT

Team Canada has consistently placed among the medal winners at the various world and Paralympic games. Highlights include a bronze medal for Canada at the 1994 winter Paralympics, another bronze at the 1996 World Championships and a silver medal at the 1998 Nagano winter Paralympics.

ATHLETE PROFILE

dean *mellway*

Key Events: Sledge hockey

Card: A

Classification: 2 IPC

Birthdate: 26/10/1949

Birthplace: Moncton, NB

Current Residence: Ottawa, ON

■ CAREER HIGHLIGHTS

Was team captain and top scorer for Canada at the 1996 Sledge Hockey World Championships in Nynashamn, Sweden (Canada captured the bronze medal at that event)

In his mid-40s, Dean Mellway is president of Canwin Sports Ltd. (a company that manufactures adapted winter-sport equipment) and co-ordinator of Physical Disability Programs at Carleton University (his full-time day job). Dean contracted polio at the age of two and has used braces, crutches or a wheelchair all his life. He is a proud member of Canada's national sledge hockey team and was team captain and top scorer for Canada at the 1996 Sledge Hockey World Championships in Nynashamn, Sweden, where Canada won the bronze medal.

Dean was first introduced to wheelchair sport in 1974, while completing his Masters degree in Social Work at Wilfrid Laurier University. He was surprised to learn that the Ontario Wheelchair Sports Association (OWSA) had been active in Hamilton and Toronto since the mid-1960s

Both as an athlete and as an organizer, Dean has contributed much to the growth of wheelchair sport.

— he had attended high school in Hamilton and had never heard anything about organized sport for people with disabilities. After competing in wheelchair sports in 1974 at the Provincial Games in Belleville and the National Games in Winnipeg, Dean set his sights on making the team and competing for Canada at the 1976 Olympiad for the Disabled in Etobicoke. He was also determined to help the organization become better known so that other young people with disabilities might become involved.

Dean was elected president of OWSA in 1975, and second vice-president of the national organization — Canadian Wheelchair Sports Association (CWSA) — in 1976. He has been involved both competitively and organizationally in sport for persons with disabilities ever since.

Both as an athlete and as an organizer, Dean has contributed much to the growth of wheelchair sport, especially in Ontario. Some of the highlights of his involvement in various organizations include:

- Founded the Twin City Spinners Wheelchair Sports Club
- Negotiated funding for the first staff positions at OWSA and the Office of Sport for the Disabled in Ontario
- Hosted the first fully integrated Provincial Basketball Championship involving wheelchair-basketball athletes and able-bodied athletes who played senior level basketball, competing in the same venue at the same time
- Organized the first National Wheelchair Basketball Championship held outside the auspices of the National Wheelchair Games
- Championed sport-specific development as executive director of the CWSA from 1981 until 1989
- Negotiated initial access to both the National Coaching Certification Program (NCCP) and Athlete Assistance Program for athletes with disabilities in all sports
- Directed CWSA through the 1980s, during which time it expanded from an annual budget of under $200,000 in 1980 to a budget of $2 million in 1989
- Assisted with the creation of the Canadian Wheelchair Basketball Association

Although Dean has clearly met and surpassed many goals, he does count a few disappointments among his triumphs. These include his withdrawal, for personal reasons, after making the 1984 Canadian wheelchair basketball team and his team's loss of the semi-final game to Norway by one goal at the 1996 World Championships. He also expresses regret over watching the stature of CWSA diminish in recent years (CWSA offices closed in 1997).

When he looks to the future, however, Dean sees hope. A recent personal athletic highlight was participating in the silver medal performance of the Canadian sledge hockey team at the 1998 Paralympics in Nagano, Japan. As for his long-range goals: "I am currently trying to support the development of sledge hockey in this country and will focus my organizational involvement on that goal," he says. "And I will always assist anyone interested in opening doors to sport for persons with disabilities."

Dean Mellway stands as a shining example of what athletes with disabilities can accomplish both on and off the field of competition.

■ Competition History

1976: Member of Canada's basketball team; gold medal in snooker and bronze medal in slalom at the Paralympiad
1977: Gold medals in snooker and slalom at Stoke Mandeville Games, England
1976-1984: Member of Canadian wheelchair basketball team
1985-1990: Two national doubles titles and one national singles title in wheelchair tennis
1989: Bronze medal at Davis Cup Competition in England
1991: Gold medal at Sledge Hockey World Cup, Oslo, Norway
1992: Gold medal at Sledge Hockey World Cup, Ottawa, ON, Canada
1994: Bronze medal at Lillehammer Paralympics in sledge hockey
1996: Bronze medal at Nynashamn, Sweden, in sledge hockey World Championships
1998: Silver medal at the Nagano winter Paralympics

SLEDGE SPEED RACING

Ice sledge speed racing is a form of speed skating in which athletes with lower limb disabilities compete. Athletes are seated on a "sledge"of fixed construction. The sledge has no steering devices and replaces skates. A cushion may be fixed to the sledge, but the sledge and cushion must not be more than 30 centimetres high at the highest point when the sledge is occupied. A seat-back of any height is permitted, and athletes may strap themselves to the sledge if they wish. Using picks similar to ski poles, athletes propel and steer the sledge during the race; they are permitted to receive a new pick during the race.

This event requires enormous upper body strength and coordination, which makes balance and speed essential to this sport. Racers compete on a standard oval speed-track of 400 metres. Windspeed indicators are used for 100 metre distances and wind speed must not exceed 1.5 metres per second in setting a World Record.

This event requires enormous upper body strength and coordination, which makes balance and speed essential to this sport.

Sledge racing is open to both males and females. Sledge racing designates two classifications of athletes with lower limb disability. The first class includes athletes who are unable to sit without support and have no significant impairment of the upper limbs. The second class of athletes are those with fair to good sitting balance. Athletes must be unable to speed skate as a direct result of their disability.

The rules that govern this sport are laid out by the International Paralympic Committee and the International Skating Union rules for speed skating. Each country can have a total of 18 competitors with a maximum of 6 per class. Both male and female sledge racers from each class participate in the following events: 100 metre, 500 metre, 700 metre and 1000 metre races. Males also participate in the 1500 metre races. In each competition, two athletes race against one another. Starting order is determined by means of a draw that takes place before the beginning of the races. Winners are declared by time — the fastest time around the track wins. If the final two athletes have identical times, both will receive the gold medal.

SWIMMING

Swimming has long been recognized as an important part of rehabilitation for people with many different types of physical injuries. It comes as no suprise, then, that many people with a physical disability who were introduced to the activitiy during the rehabilitation process became enamoured with the sport and pursued it to national and international levels.

In recent years the popularity of swimming as a sport amongst people with mobility impairments has grown in proportion to the increasing number of wheelchair-accessible pools. Most swimming facilities have been built in the last 20 years and are therefore

Andrew Haley competing at the 1996 Paralympics in Atlanta.

accessible to most people with a disability. After they are taught how to swim, only those people with the most severe disabilities require aids or support. As well, facilities are available in almost every community, and swimming is not an expensive activity. Most important of all, the organizations involved with swimming, such as Swim Canada, actively include people with disabilities in their sport.

Many people with mobility impairments who swim at the recreational level do so because the activity gives them an incredible feeling of cheating gravity. The feelings associated with gravity, ever-present on dry land, disappear immediately when a person enters water. People with even the most severe physical restrictions on dry land find themselves able to move their bodies with relative ease once they are in the pool.

> *Organizations involved with swimming, such as Swim Canada, actively include people with disabilities in their sport.*

One of the more progressive movements in Canadian sport in the last several years has been the inclusion of athletes with a disability in the programs of Swim Canada. Before 1992, swimmers with a disability were a major part of disability sport groups such as the Canadian Wheelchair Sports Association and the Canadian Amputee Sports Association. But in recent years, swimmers with amputations, those who are paraplegics and those who have visual impairments or cerebral palsy are now integrated into the non-disabled sport structure of Swim Canada.

The movement toward the inclusion of athletes with a disability into non-disabled sport groups has been an initiative of the federal government (in order to decrease duplication of services) and by the Commission for Inclusion of Athletes with a Disability (CIAD), which is chaired by wheelchair athlete Rick Hansen.

Although there have been some growing pains in the inclusion movement, Canada has led the way among the world's nations in their inclusion of athletes with a disability into the able-bodied sport structure. One of the main attractions of competitive swimming for people with a disability is the Canadian masters program. Unlike many other sports, where the masters category begins at age 40, in swimming the masters category starts at the age of 18. The masters program enables people of all abilities to compete against others with similar abilities, thus giving swimmers with a disability the opportunity to swim with other swimmers of similar capabilities, disabled or otherwise.

■ SPORT HIGHLIGHT

The highlight of the inclusion movement was at the 1994 Commonwealth Games in Victoria, BC. Millions of viewers across the world watched Nova Scotia's amputee swimmer Andrew Haley inch out Australia's Brendan Burkett for a gold medal finish in the men's 100-metre freestyle. The success of Andrew Haley at the Commonwealth Games represented everything the swimming movement in Canada was hoping to accomplish. Andrew trains with the university club at Dalhousie University in Halifax.

ATHLETE PROFILE

rebeccah *bornemann*

Key Event: swimming (freestyle 50 metres to 400 metres)

Card: retired

Classification: S7, SB7, M7

Birthdate: 17/06/1972

Birthplace: Sharon, CT

Current Residence: Edmonton, AB

■ CAREER HIGHLIGHT

Member 1996 Paralympic swim team; won gold in 400m freestyle, came 4th in 100m free and 6th in 50m free

Rebeccah Bornemann has been part of a new generation of athletes with a disability in Canada — athletes who have risen through the ranks of an integrated class system, integrated training and an integrated competition system via Swim Natation Canada (SNC).

While a significant number of Canadian swimmers with disabilities had unofficially trained and competed with non-disability swim clubs for years, it was not until 1993, when a "memorandum of understanding" (MOU) was signed between Swim Canada and the various disability sport organizations, that swimmers with disabilities became fully integrated into SNC. A shining example of this co-operation was the 1994 Commonwealth Games in Victoria, where athletes with a disability and those without competed together — and against each other — for the first time ever in Canada. Rebeccah Bornemann is one of the first graduates of this inclusive system.

Rebeccah currently studies at the University of Alberta, home of the world-renowned Rick Hansen Centre and International Paralympic Committee president Dr. Robert

Steadward. Here is Rebeccah's story, in her own words:

My name is Rebeccah Bornemann. I am 25 years old and have recently retired from competitive sport. I am working on my master's degree in sport psychology with a particular focus on integration (cross-disability and disabled/able-bodied). I am also an assistant coach with the University of Alberta swim team.

I have had cerebral palsy since birth and I didn't get involved with sport until I was in my early teens. My family has always been quite physically active; they treated me like a "normal child" — so much so that it was not until I was 11 or 12 that I realized *intellectually* that I had a disability. I knew that I was different, but up until then I had never labelled myself — and anyway, I knew that everyone was different somehow. At this point I had some really negative experiences in Phys Ed class at school and in a therapeutic horseback riding program. The combination of these two experiences left me feeling as though I was trapped inside a body that didn't work (typical teenage angst with a zinger!), and I had some pretty negative self-image and self-esteem problems. To cope with this, I divided the two parts of myself into the intellectual me on the one hand, and the disabled me who became involved in sport on the other. It took me a while to realize that I had done this, as I went to great lengths to keep the two parts of my life separate. I've spent just as many years since trying to reintegrate the pieces.

> *"The most momentous thing I have ever done has concerned integrating myself — something that I've done consciously and deliberately."*

It was in the fall of 1986 when I was 14 that I started participating in a swimming program run by the Nova Scotia Canadian Wheelchair Sports Association (CWSA-NS). We lived in Halifax at the time and this was the only disability sport organization with any money and, therefore, formal programming. I remember that my mother made me go — I think in desperation — and told me that I only had to go once. I had really enjoyed swimming as a child and had plodded through all the Red Cross badges, persevering to the end. Anyway, I met a wonderful woman named Sue McLeod there; she seemed genuinely impressed with my swimming abilities and was quite encouraging. So I went back.

I didn't actually go to my first meet until 1988, when we went to the Windsor Classic Indoor Games. The cerebral palsy swim-team manager, Doug Wilton, was there and he was also encouraging. I remember that he said something about me having national team potential; suddenly I had a tangible goal to work towards and I set myself to the task with a venegence. As well, Seoul Paralympian Jamie Bone used to come to the pool for fun (he was a wheelchair sprinter), and I admired his dedication on the track and wanted to share being a part of the Paralympian dream. I was hooked.

The most momentous thing I have ever done has concerned integrating myself — something that I've done consciously and deliberately, and in a major way, three times. When I started at Smith College in 1990 I knew that if I wanted to swim, my only real option was to swim with the able-bodied team. (Swimming did not really enter into my decision to go to Smith; I was still segregating my life at that time, and it was a purely academic choice).

So, absolutely terrified, I went to the coach, Kim Bierwert, and explained that I wanted to swim but "I...I, uh, have this, um, like, um, a disability thing." He said that he did not cut anyone from the team, that people cut themselves. I don't think that I have ever heard such a simultaneously reassuring and utterly horrifying statement. I swam the first year, scared, certain that everyone was looking at me and wondering what the heck I was doing there. In my second year, when I finally felt comfortable enough to actually talk to people, I found that their reaction was different than I had thought it would be. They were impressed that, despite my physical limitations, I did the same workouts and that I worked so hard.

Kim Bierwert was really good about giving me the kinds of workouts that I needed, and he really pushed and challenged me. I remember that he would sometimes put me in events if he thought that it would be a close race for me. As a result, I occasionally ended up "beating" able-bodied swimmers, which would give me moments of wonderful quiet satisfaction (and this was probably the point, beyond giving me practice in "swimming tough").

After the Barcelona Paralympics, I took a year off school and spent the time with my family in Vancouver. Again, the best training option was with an able-bodied club. (This was before the MOU was signed and integration was not yet officially sanctioned). I called the Pacific Dolphin Swim Association and started off swimming with their age-group program. However, through a combination of the swimmers being much younger than I and what I perceived as the coach's less-than-helpful attitude, I did not feel at all comfortable with that group. So I contacted Tom Johnson, who was the head of their top program (he's also an Olympic/national team coach). I explained to him, knees knocking, that I was a double bronze medallist at an international games and that I wanted to have the same calibre of training as my able-bodied peers. He said he'd think about it; I wouldn't be at all surprised to learn that he was as uncomfortable with me at that moment as I was with him. By the next day, though, he had thought things through and had a justification in his mind for letting me on the team. And so I started training with Tom, which I would do during non-academic portions of the following years. Over time we became more comfortable with each other and worked well together. It has been a real privilege for me to be able to work with Tom.

The third time that I integrated myself was when I came to the University of Alberta. I have been very lucky to have found another wonderful coach, Deb Sigaty, with whom (I am glad to say) I am now working as an assistant coach. The third time was eas*ier*, although still not easy! For this reason, I would say that my biggest accomplishments have been the personal ones.

■ COMPETITION HISTORY

1989: National (CP) team member and medallist at first Robin Hood Games, Nottingham, England; medallist, Foresters' Games, Richmond, BC

1990: National (CP) team member and competitor at World Championships, Assen

1991: Medallist, Foresters' Games, Brantford, ON; selected to (CP) Paralympic Shadow Team (functional classification)

1992: Demo events at SNC winter Nationals in Winnepeg, MB; IX Paralympic Games, Barcelona, Spain — won bronze medal in 400 metre freestyle (S8) and 100 metre freestyle (S8), and came fourth in 50 metre freestyle; set new Canadian records

1993: Medallist, Foresters' Games/Swimming Nationals, Halifax, NS; set world record in 200 metre butterfly (S8) at Ontario Provincials; participated in demonstration events at SNC Nationals in Edmonton

1994: Medallist, Commonwealth trials, Victoria, BC (100 metre freestyle); medallist, first SNC Swimmers with a Disability (SWAD) championships, Winnipeg, MB; member, Commonwealth Games team — came seventh in 100 metre freestyle (swam "up" in S9); member of SNC team to first International Paralympic Committee (IPC) Swimming Championships in Malta — came fourth in 400 metre freestyle (S8), fifth in 100 metre freestyle and 100 metre fly, sixth in 50 metre freestyle

1995: Medallist, SWAD Nationals, Lethbridge, AB; member of SNC team to Atlanta Invitational Swim Meet — won gold in 400 metre freestyle (S7) and 100 metre freestyle (S7), and silver in 50 metre freestyle (S7)

1996: Medallist, SWAD Nationals, Nepean, ON; member Paralympic swim team in Atlanta — won gold in 400 metre freestyle (S7), came fourth in 100 metre freestyle and sixth in 50 metre freestyle

■ COMMITTEE AND COACHING INVOLVEMENT

1993: Athlete representative to the Canadian Cerebral Palsy Sports Association (CCPSA) swimming technical committee

1993-1996: Elected athlete representative at Nationals to Committee for Swimmers with a Disability, which integrated with Swim Natation Canada and was recently disbanded in favour of a more integrated approach within the SNC structure. The memorandum of understanding to this effect was signed with SNC in June 1994

1995-96: Swimming representative and chair of the Canadian Paralympic Committee's (CPC) newly formed athletes' council, which has a liaison to board of Canadian Athletes' Association (now called Athletes CAN)

1998: Working on coaching certification and classification certification

ATHLETE PROFILE

walter *wu*

Key Event: Swimming

Card: A

Classification: B3

Birthdate: 1973

Birthplace: Richmond, BC

Current Residence: Richmond, BC

PHOTO: *Walter Wu (centre) shows his gold medal at the 1996 Paralympics in Atlanta.*

■ **CAREER HIGHLIGHT**

At the November 1994 Swimming World Championships in Malta, Wu slashed the previous world record for the Men's B3 category in the 200-metre individual medley event, and received four gold medals and a silver medal

C anada's top visually impaired swimmer is 26-year-old Walter Wu. Up until five years ago, Wu had never competed as a "disabled" swimmer. In fact, it was not until the age of 17 that Wu realized he was legally blind.

"My father popped into the local Canadian National Institute for the Blind (CNIB) to see what was available there," he remembers. "They suggested that I go in to see them and get my vision tested. They told me I was legally blind at that point. My eyesight hadn't changed over the years, my parents just didn't realise the extent of my visual impairment."

Walter's parents introduced him to swimming at the age of seven at their local swimming club in Richmond, BC. At age 12 he transferred to the Dolphins club, which was based out of the Vancouver Aquatic Centre. While he was with this club, he got to swim with the University of British Columbia (UBC) Thunderbirds swim team. Walter noticed a big difference between swimming with a varsity team and the local club scene.

Once Walter was categorized as legally blind, it didn't take long for the local BC Blind Sports Association to track him down and recruit him for the national team. Walter began to get involved in swimming from the perspective of a swimmer with a disability. "I first became involved in blind sports in 1990 and competed at local levels and then the nationals," he relates.

At the Atlanta Paralympics in 1996, Wu won five gold medals and set five world records.

At the November 1994 Swimming World Championships in Malta, Wu slashed the previous world record for the men's B3 category in the 200-metre individual medley event and received four gold medals and a silver medal in the process. And at the Atlanta Paralympics in 1996, Wu won five gold medals and set five world records. Swimming at the international level has also had positive social effects on the Richmond native. "I certainly got to experience different cultures at the World Championship in Malta and at the Paralympics," he says.

Walter Wu is a perfect example of how swimmers with a disability can fit right in to the non-disabled sport structure.

TRACK and FIELD (ATHLETICS)

T raditionally, track and field has been the most popular sport for people with disabilities, not only in Canada but also in the rest of the world.

Athletes using wheelchairs, runners missing various limbs, throwers without sight and jumpers who cannot hear are all capable of competing in athletics at a very high level. Indeed, it was the idea of athletes using wheelchairs to race each other that resulted in track becoming the first sport to be included in the early Paralympics. Similarly, throwing the discus and javelin from wheelchairs proved very popular among athletes with disabilities in the 1950s.

Over the years, track and field events for people with other disabilities — athletes who were amputees, blind or partially sighted, or who had cerebral palsy — became increasingly popular. Unfortunately, Canada has yet to see a combined national athletic championship that encompasses all disability and non-disability groups. The wheelchair athletes have successfully merged themselves with Athletics Canada, but the struggle continues for athletes who are blind, who are amputees or who have cerebral palsy. They strive to maintain a national championship event every two years.

Athletics Canada has made some inroads in increasing the profile of the sport by adopting elite wheelchair athletes such as Jeff Adams and Chantal Petitclerc.

Marathons and road races for wheelchair athletes continue to be popular, and track and field events for athletes with disabilities continue to attract participants, although lack of general public support for the sport has affected the growth in both disability and non-disability events. The generally conservative Athletics Canada has made some inroads in increasing the profile of the sport by adopting elite wheelchair athletes such as Jeff Adams and Chantal Petitclerc. As well, the existence of wheelchair demonstration events at the Olympics, Commonwealth Games and World Championships has furthered the cause for wheelchair athletes worldwide. Still, athletes who are amputees, blind or belong to other disability groups have yet to be similarly recognized.

Even with the current limitations, Canada has provided some incredible track and field athletes to various events over the years. Quebec's Andre Viger and Jacques Martin, Manitoba's Arnold Boldt, Newfoundland's Mel Fitzgerald and Ontario's Jeff Tiessen and Joanne Bouw have all reached the pinnacle of achievement within the sport.

■ SPORT HIGHLIGHT

Canadian track and field highlights include Arnold Boldt's incredible one-legged high jump of 2.05 metres, which sadly goes unrecognised even today because the International Amateur Athletic Federation (IAAF) meet at which the record was set was not sanctioned by the International Sports Organization for the Disabled (ISOD). Another Canadian highlight occurred when Jeff Adams won gold medals at the 1994 Commonwealth Games and at the 1995 IAAF World Championships in Sweden.

Bruce Russell throwing the discus.

jeff adams

Key Events: Wheelchair athletics (1500 metres)

Card: A

Classification: T4

Birthdate: 15/11/1970

Birthplace: Mississauga, ON

Current Residence: Toronto, ON

PHOTO: *Jeff Adams at the 1995 IAAF World Championships.*

■ CAREER HIGHLIGHT

Gold medal at the 1995 IAAF World Championships in the 1500 metre race

M any Canadians had an unforgettable introduction to Jeff Adams during his athletic performance at the 1992 Barcelona Olympics in the 1500 metre wheelchair event. Although he experienced a mechanical failure during the race, Adams' performance showed millions of people that athletes with a disability are prone to dramatic successes and failures, just like all athletes. To make amends, Adams snatched victory from defeat at the first-ever 1500 metre wheelchair event at the International Amateur Athletic Federation (IAAF) World Championships in Goteborg, Sweden, in 1995.

Adams' outspoken views on disability sport in Canada have cost him financially and lost him sponsorships, but he continues to criticize the very sport that has brought him to public attention. He expressed some of his thoughts on wheelchair sports and disability in general during the following conversation with the author.

Jeff, how do you feel about the continued "exhibition" status for wheelchair athletics, especially given the men's 800 metre wheelchair race was not an official event at the last Commonwealth Games, and nor was the recent 1500 metre race

at the IAAF World Championships in Goteborg, Sweden?

I don't think we should have an official event until the able-bodied compete in wheelchairs. I don't think we should have any segregated events at elite competitions such as the Commonwealth Games or World Championships or Olympics. It doesn't fit with the philosophy and the direction of the games and what the games are all about. I don't have a problem with not receiving a medal because there are no able-bodied athletes competing in wheelchair events. Until the sport is a pure sport and is open to the entire world's population, like any of the other sports, we shouldn't have official medals.

I don't see this event [wheelchair racing] as a wheelchair sport anymore; it is a sport first and foremost. There are two factors that are important for an elite athlete: one is that you are graced with a physical ability; the second is that you make the most of that physical ability and work with it. I think the uniqueness of wheelchair sport is that we have an implement that allows us to "reverse integrate" and also to lessen our disability to the point where we can compete against the able-bodied. It is unfortunate, but it is also a reality that you can't reverse integrate in all of the disability groups. For example, you can't — without some radical surgical procedures — reverse integrate in amputee events.

You can't draw a thin line in discriminating between disabilities. It takes a thick fuzzy line to determine who has a disability and who doesn't. In reality, 90 percent of the world's population has some kind of disability. If you are born with slow-twitch fibres, that's a disability if you want to become a 100-metre runner. It's a reality that a lot of people have to live with. Personally, I don't discriminate between a person who is born short and a person who is born with no legs.

I don't think the level of competition is necessarily the same in the other disability groups as it is between wheelchair racers. I don't mean to be calling down any individual athlete, but a lot of the members of the Canadian National Team don't train as hard as the able-bodied do and as I do. I know that all the wheelchair racers who were in Barcelona do train as hard as the able-bodied.

Every time I go out and train with an athlete with cerebral palsy who is in a wheelchair and who starts a 400 metre run and finishes it at the 200 metre mark, I have to scratch my head at that. If you train for the 400 metres, you know you don't stop at 200 metres. So there's a huge, huge gap between some of the athletes at disabled events and that is what I object to. People are going to World Championships and are coming home with medals when there are only two people in their event. The women's shot-put event for the blind in Berlin was a prime example of this. Ljiljana Ljubisic is a B1; she got bumped up to a B2 and she still won the discus and placed second in the shot-put. Where is Ljubisic's disability if she can go out and beat a whole class above her?

> **"I don't think we should have an official event until the able-bodied compete in wheelchairs."**

There are too many athletes competing in as many events as humanly possible. The field athletes at the Commonwealth Games don't throw the three throwing events. Every standing cerebral palsy athlete I know throws in every throwing event. Every blind thrower throws three implements. Among amputees, some runners who compete in the sprinting events just don't have the build or the genetics of a sprinter. People find it difficult to take a sport seriously when it involves competitors who don't look right for the event. To be that much of an all-round athlete is silly. The days when you could do that in non-disabled sports are long gone, and it is time the athletes with disabilities started to specialize.

I don't think we should have official events in the Olympics right now, especially because we don't have the able-bodied competing against us. We have to go through a final maturing process before we can have an official event. None of the other disability groups can do that because of the nature of their disabilities. I don't know if any of the other groups can present a logical argument as to why they should be at the Olympics. Everyone wants to talk about why a disabled person should be at the Olympics, but there is nothing stopping the athletes with a disability from competing at local twilight meets. They should have the exact same opportunities as my neighbour — who is five feet, two inches tall — to go to the Olympics. I disagree that we have the right to progress past my neighbour, who may have equally disadvantaged circumstances.

ATHLETE PROFILE

arnold boldt

Key Events: High jump, long jump, volleyball

Card: Never carded

Classification: A2

Birthplace: Osler, SK

Current Residence: Thomson, MB

PHOTO: *Arnold Boldt circa 1980, at the height of his career.*

■ CAREER HIGHLIGHT

Set a world record in the high jump in 1981 that still holds today

In a career that spanned almost 20 years, Arnold Boldt was the epitome of the dedicated athlete with a disability, successful in both disability sport and sport at the collegiate level through the Canadian Intercollegiate Athletic Union (CIAU). Today, Boldt is in a perfect position to analyze the pros and cons of the disability sport movement over the past two decades.

Arnold Boldt was born near Osler, Saskatchewan and lived there for his first 12 years. He then lived in Abbotsford, BC, for two years, moved back to Osler, back to Abbotsford, and then lived in Saskatoon, Winnipeg, Quebec City and Vancouver. Arnold began to be involved in sport at a very early age. In elementary school he found that he had an interest in track and field, and in Grade Three, at age nine, he started to develop a particular interest in the high jump and the standing long jump.

Boldt carved practice areas out of the prairie, using diesel fuel to clear areas. He set up high-jump stands with two-by-fours, and jumped into sand pits or onto bales of hay. He even set up a high-jump area in his parents' basement, landing on a couch. During these early years, Arnold lived in a farming community where physical injury was fairly commonplace, and he encountered nothing but positive support for his drive to pursue athletic endeavours. "I was fairly well accepted for who I was," he says. "It was quite easy to be yourself and do what you wanted to do without people prejudging you."

Through prosthetist Stan Holcomb, Arnold discovered sport for amputees. In 1976, when he was 18, he competed for Canada at the Toronto Paralympiad and received his first gold medal. During this time he was also playing wheelchair basketball in the Saskatoon area. Disability sport answered his growing need to compete with other amputees. "I'd dreamed about having an event that put me on equal footing with others," he remembers. In this way, the teenaged Arnold Boldt was part of the early days in Canadian amputee sports. "There were a lot of young and very enthusiastic people around in 1976. There were a lot of amputees around at that time who were very keen. We were all strictly amateurs — we had no formal training."

Arnie was approached by the Canadian Broadcasting Corporation (CBC) in 1977 to work on the script for the movie *Crossbar* which was "very loosely" based on Boldt's career as a high jumper. From then on Boldt established himself as the world's top amputee high jumper, garnering invitations to both disability sport and able-bodied track meets all over the world.

In the late 1970s, Boldt attended the University of Saskatchewan and University of Manitoba and competed for the track team in the high jump at the CIAU level. "My best performances came at these meets, probably because it was the right time of year. I found it difficult to train for the disability sport meets through the summer because I had to work. I believe in the theory if you are an average

Boldt in Edmonton, 1979.

athlete and you compete against someone better, you will always perform better than when you compete against someone who is not as good as you. My best performance in an outdoor disabled/amputee meet was in 1981 in Italy with a jump of 2.04 metres. My best indoor performance was at the Tribune Games in Winnipeg in 1981 with a jump of 2.08 metres. My average CIAU performance was always over 2 metres."

Boldt has seen many changes in the disability sport movement in the last 20 years. "The quality of the training and the dedication of the athletes has really improved. People take things a lot more seriously, especially at the international level."

Despite the increased dedication of the athletes, Arnie notes that other factors have contributed to the rise and fall in popularity of Canadian disability sport. "There was a high point of enthusiasm in Canada around 1976, especially regarding media recognition of disability sport, and it seems to have tapered ever since."

Boldt believes the survival of disability sport (at least for amputees) in Canada will be directly related to investment in the development of younger athletes. "The nurturing of new athletes and new blood has been lacking," he warns. Boldt is also disturbed that federal funding for athletes with disabilities was only made available in the last two years of his 18-year career. "I applied for federal funding many times and was turned down for one reason or another. Maybe CASA [the Canadian Amputee Sports Association] didn't have the right forms or the right connections in Ottawa. It's not as if we didn't give anything back to the country either. Some of us would have done a lot better, stayed with the program longer and been a little more intense about the whole thing; this would have inspired a lot of younger kids to come along. There is still a lack of a federal program that brings along athletes in combination with the development of employment or educational skills."

"It always blew me away that I was more famous in Europe than I was in Canada."

Arnie also feels that the progress of Canadian athletes with disabilities suffers because the athletes lack recognition from indifferent track and field audiences. "It always blew me away that I was more famous in Europe than I was in Canada," he says. "I went to Italy almost a dozen times and I'd walk down the street after each meet and get mobbed."

Today, Arnold Boldt is focussed on the future. He and his peers realize the continued development of Canadian disability sport is dependent on the ability of various organizations to find and nurture the new and younger athletes. "If there is going to be a future for Canadian disability sport we really need to bring along the younger athletes," he says.

In the meantime, Arnold's world and Paralympic high jump record — set in 1980 — still stands at 1.96 metres.

ATHLETE PROFILE

Ljiljana *ljubisic*

Key Events: Shot-put, discus

Card: A

Classification: B2

Birthplace: Yugoslavia

Current Residence: Coquitlam, BC

■ CAREER HIGHLIGHT

Participated in the Paralympics in Seoul in 1988 and Barcelona in 1992

Ljiljana Ljubisic was born in Yugoslavia but grew up in British Columbia's lower mainland. While they were still living in Yugoslavia, Ljiljana's parents went to the Supreme Court in order to keep their young daughter out of institutions for the blind; they were successful. Both parents were stellar athletes within their sports of basketball and rowing in their native Yugoslavia. Ljiljana's older brother was a National Collegiate Athletic Association (NCAA) football player. Ljiljana grew up in an environment of sport and was encouraged from an early age to be active.

Ljiljana graduated from Centennial High School in Coquitlam, BC, in 1979. She was one of the few blind kids in the mainstream school system (most blind children did not have access to mainstream classes until 1979). "I was somewhat misunderstood by teachers and students while I was in

Ljiljana Ljubisic competing in the 1989 Canadian Games.

high school because I was invisibly disabled," remembers Ljiljana. "I was very light sensitive. I used dark glasses and I had to put my nose into my book. This caused me to be somewhat outcast by my peers — besides being five feet and eleven inches tall by the age of 13."

Despite her athletic background, Ljiljana too often found herself being shipped off to the library during gym class. This antiquated practice engendered feelings of rejection in Ljiljana and erected further barriers between Ljiljana and her fellow students. "I was never encouraged to be active in sport through the school system," she recalls. It was only upon returning home at the end of every school day that Ljiljana's physical abilities were allowed to shine — she would relieve her frustrations by playing ball on the basketball court in the driveway.

As Ljiljana's sight deteriorated she began to realize no one in her immediate circle was going to be able to help her as much as she needed. So, with the assistance of her brother, Ljiljana learned to ski through the Disabled Skiers Association of British Columbia (DSABC) program on Grouse Mountain in Vancouver in the winter of 1981-82. Shortly after this, Ljiljana was introduced to sport for the blind by Matt Salli. They met while she was training in the gym at the University of British Columbia. Salli immediately recognized Ljubisic's height advantage for the sport of goalball. He recommended Ljiljana to the provincial team in 1982.

"I fell passionately in love with the sport of goalball almost immediately," says Ljiljana. "It filled a void in me. At the time I didn't have the confidence to compete in an individual event, so this team sport really helped me develop confidence as an athlete." Ljiljana helped the BC team win its first ever gold medal at a national championship in Calgary in 1984. Later that same year Ljiljana was chosen for the national team and went on to claim a silver medal at the International Games for the Disabled in New York.

After the New York games, Ljiljana's overall athletic talent was recognized by the Canadian Blind Sports Association (CBSA) and she was exposed to several new sports. Two of those sports — shot-put and discus — caught Ljiljana's attention. Having gained confidence in a team sport, Ljiljana felt prepared to tackle the individual sports of discus and shot-put. "The feeling of being able to thrust something so far into the air was very appealing to me," she says. "I didn't outgrow team sports; I got a little tired of the politics and crap that came along with them. I'm a very independent person and this pulled me toward the discus and shot-put. Plus I didn't have to play any political games — I didn't have to kiss anybody's ass to get on the team or stay on the court. I didn't have to justify to anyone why I scored all the goals and they didn't. The politics of team sports got to me at the right time."

I'm an athlete at heart. Whether I was blind, paralyzed or not disabled at all, I would still be involved in a high level of sport."

Ljiljana soon connected with a coach who knew about shot-put and discus throws and was able to put in the one-on-one training time with her. From then on, Ljiljana trained five or six days a week and found herself on the road to Seoul in 1988 and Barcelona in 1992. "It takes a different kind of ego to stand out there in the circle," she says. "When you fail it's your failure and when you win it is all your glory."

Ljiljana describes part of the joy and attraction of her chosen sports this way: "At one point the sun reflected off the discus and with my limited sight I saw the implement flying through the air. This gave me a powerful feeling and I was hooked. I'm an athlete at heart. Whether I was blind, paralyzed or not disabled at all, I would still be involved in a high level of sport."

Competing at the international level has left Ljiljana with some reservations regarding ongoing developments for athletes with disabilities at the international level. "Over the years the opportunity for people to compete with others at the same level of disability has been eroded in a very dramatic way. I'm starting to experience an erosion of opportunities. The Paralympics are becoming an event for those of us with the least amount of disability and not an event for those with the most disability. Even world record holders are being shoved into extinction because of their level of disability and the class they are in."

In Ljiljana's opinion, the international classification system is at the root of the problem faced by athletes at all levels. "The classification system is becoming a huge problem. The B1s, the low-functioning athletes with cerebral palsy and the quadriplegics are more and more becoming athletes who should be on the 'endangered' list at the Paralympic and World Championship level.

"The standards that are being set for entry qualification into the Paralympic and World meets are far too high when based on a percentage of the world record. When the world record was reset to 46 metres in my discus event by a B2 thrower who had previously competed at the collegiate level as a sighted thrower, the next closest distance was six metres less. Setting the entry standard at 85 percent of the world record excludes an extraordinary number of athletes. In turn, we are told we have to join other classes because there are not enough athletes within my class to provide a decent competitive event. The entry standard should be set by taking into account the best results of the top eight athletes rather than by figuring out a percentage of a world record. By using percentages we are eliminating whole classes of women from several sports."

In looking to the future, Ljiljana believes that the Paralympics will develop in a manner somewhat parallel to the Olympics, although, she says, we are not yet at the stage where the two movements can combine as one. "Overall, we have to figure out what our mission is. I don't think at this point we have a clear mandate at all levels of disability sport. We really have to have our own house in order before we can develop successful relationships with the Commonwealth Games and the International Olympic Committee."

ATHLETE PROFILE

chantal
petitclerc

Key Event: Wheelchair athletics (200 metres, 400 metres, 800 metres, 1500 metres)

Card: "A"

Classification: T4

Birthdate: 15/12/1969

Birthplace: Ste-Foy, QC

Current Residence: Montreal, QC

■ CAREER HIGHLIGHT

In 1995 won five gold medals at the Stoke Mandeville Wheelchair Games

Chantal Petitclerc's consistency internationally has made her the first Canadian female star in the sport of wheelchair athletics. In the summer of 1995, Chantal won five gold medals at the Stoke Mandeville Wheelchair Games as well as the silver medal in the 800 metre event at the International Amateur Athletics Federation (IAAF) World Championships.

Versatility has always been one of Chantal's strengths. She currently holds the Canadian women's record in the 100-metre, 200-metre, 400-metre, 800-metre and 1500-metre events. She also holds the best time recorded by a Canadian woman in the marathon.

By her own admission, Chantal was not particularly involved in sports during her childhood. It was not until 1988, five years after the accident that had left her a paraplegic, that she tried wheelchair racing for the first time. Pierre Pomerleau, the wheelchair coach for the Quebec City region, gave Chantal the itch to compete. She participated in a number of provincial competitions, met the standard to compete at the Canadian championships and, at the end of the 1988 season, was chosen as rookie of the year in wheelchair sports — not a bad beginning for a woman who didn't begin training as an athlete until her twentieth year.

Since then, Chantal has travelled down many roads. A determined person, Chantal knows where she's headed and does everything necessary to get there. Her most recent challenge was participating in the Olympic Games in Atlanta, where the 800-metre race in wheelchair athletics was a demonstration event. "The Olympic Games are important to me," explains Chantal. "That's where all the media are and the public; that's where our sport can become better known. We can't hide, and wheelchair sports is still not very well known."

"The visibility of my sport is not great, but it's not a question of prejudice. It's more a problem of education."

Chantal is not only an exceptional athlete, she is also an exceptional role model. As a host for Lotto Quebec, she brings the image of an athlete who uses a wheelchair into millions of homes every week. Aside from training for 25 hours each week and working in the evenings, she also finds the time to be honourary chair for the Women's March Against Poverty — a project dear to her heart.

The insurance company and corporate sponsor MetLife recently recognized Chantal's accomplishments — she was one of only four athletes with a disability chosen to receive a MetLife bursary in preparation for the 1998 Olympics and Paralympics in Atlanta. As a result, Petitclerc paraded beside her fellow Canadian Olympians in Atlanta and earned two gold medals, in the 200 metres and the 400 metres, as well as a bronze in the 800 metres. Her performance delighted her and she described it as the best moment of her career. "I really wanted those medals. In the past I had only succeeded in winning bronze medals in international competitions. I trained really hard for these championships. I was very confident. This time I felt that my time had come and I was going to win. It was imprinted in large black letters in my head."

"I am an athlete, like all the others," Chantal strongly insists. She considers herself to be a serious athlete and, as such, would like to compete on the same level as her able-bodied counterparts — and not only in competitions reserved for the disabled. That is why, despite her desire to remain versatile as an athlete, she recently focussed her preparation on the 800-metre demonstration event at the Olympic Games.

As a trained athlete, Chantal realizes that she must continue to improve. "The main quality of an athlete is to never be satisfied," she says, laughing. " I still have work to do on my strength and I have to improve my mental preparation before a competition."

Chantal feels lucky to be living in Quebec, where, she believes, the environment for athletes with a disability is excellent. "Obviously, the visibility of my sport is not great, but it's not a question of prejudice. It's more a problem of education. You can't forget that, in other countries, wheelchair athletes are considered to be a class below other athletes. Luckily, that is not the case here."

ATHLETE PROFILE

eugene
reimer

Key Events: Wheelchair athletics; basketball; swimming; powerlifting

Card: never carded

Classification: 5 IMSWF

Birthplace: Abbotsford, BC

Current Residence: Abbotsford, BC

PHOTO: *Eugene Reimer throwing the javelin in 1975.*

■ CAREER HIGHLIGHT

Won the Canadian Male Athlete of the Year Award in 1973

Before Jeff Adams was even a twinkle in his parents' eyes and when Rick Hansen was just a lad fishing the rivers around Williams Lake, Abbotsford native Eugene Reimer was hauling in medals from various international disability sport events.

In 1973 Eugene Reimer was honoured with the prestigious Canadian Male Athlete of the Year Award.

Gene first became involved in disability sport just after the 1967 Pan American Games in Winnipeg. In 1968 he competed in Tel Aviv, Israel, at Canada's first ever Paralympic event and dominated the events he entered. In those days the athletes could compete in all the events. Gene excelled in track and field, basketball, swimming and powerlifting. In fact, he dominated Canadian wheelchair sport in these events until his retirement in 1981.

In 1973 Eugene Reimer was honoured with the prestigious Canadian Male Athlete of the Year Award (Karen Magnussen won the women's award). It is interesting to note that no athlete with a disability has won the award since (although Arnie Boldt was runner-up to Greg Joy in 1976).

In the late 1960s and throughout the 1970s Gene Reimer represented the peak performance among athletes involved with Canadian disability sport. Today Gene operates a building supply shop in Abbotsford, BC, where he lives with his family.

ATHLETE PROFILE

andre
viger

Key Events: Wheelchair athletics (5000 metres; 10 kilometres; marathon)

Card: "A"

Classification: T4

Birthdate: 27/09/1952

Birthplace: Windsor, ON

Residence: Montreal, QC

Andre Viger has been one of Canada's most successful wheelchair athletes since he began competing in 1979. Today, in his 40s, he refuses to slow down. In addition to a host of other impressive international achievements, he has recently won marathons in Boston, Paris and Oita, Japan.

During his career, Andre has won almost every major marathon and has held world records in the marathon and the 800-metre, 1500-metre and 10,000-metre events. In 1984 he won the bronze medal in the 1,500-metre demonstration event at the Los Angeles Olympics. In 1988, in Seoul, he won the marathon event, placed second in the 10,000 metres and finished third in the 5,000-metre and 800-metre races. His success continued at the Paralympic Games in Barcelona in 1992, where, in addition to bringing home three medals, he also set two Canadian records. In 1996 Andre participated in the Paralympic Games for the fifth time in his career.

Andre has won almost every major marathon and has held world records.

Today, Andre is still going strong. He has no special formula for his lasting success except hard work and dedication to the sport. In the world of wheelchair sports, Andre is known as "The King of the Road" — the athlete who takes every race as a new challenge and is always inspired to do his best.

■ AWARDS

Outstanding Young People in the World (1985)
Quebec Athlete of the Year (1985)
Government of Canada Sport Excellence Award (1985)
King Clancy Award (1991)
Stan Stronge Memorial Award (1994)

WHEELCHAIR BASKETBALL

In many ways, the story of wheelchair basketball is the story of sport for people with disabilities in Canada and elsewhere. In the western world, basketball was the first sport to be played by people with serious physical impairments that could only be overcome by using a wheelchair.

After the Second World War, society was confronted by an unusually high number of people — many of them young — with physical disabilities. These people let the world know that they had needs beyond food, clothing and shelter. They had egos, they were worthwhile and they belonged — in short, they were part of society.

The philosophy of the day was for rehabilitation staff to adapt particular sports to the needs of their patients and clients. Basketball was perceived to be one of the most adaptable team sports and was played by people with disabilities in various parts of the world by the early 1940s. Then, in 1944, Sir Ludwig Guttmann was given the task of establishing a spinal cord injuries centre at Stoke Mandeville Hospital in Aylesbury, Buckinghamshire, England. The British government funded the operation. The goal was to assist individuals in coping with their disabilities and regaining the dignity and independence they may have lost so that they could become happy, healthy and respected members of the community. The Stoke Mandeville World Wheelchair Games in 1948 marked the beginning of organized wheelchair sports and earned Sir Ludwig Guttmann the distinction of becoming a founding father of sports for people in wheelchairs.

The story of wheelchair basketball is the story of sport for people with disabilities in Canada and elsewhere.

In Canada there were similar developments. In 1947 the Deer Lodge Hospital in Manitoba organized an event on the front lawn of its facility. A basketball throw accompanied events like the ring toss, milk-bottle pitching, archery, croquet and golf putting. Luci Delucca was one of the organizers of that event; participants included George Dyck, Joe Smithson and Tony Mann. The events had a rehabilitative aim and were mostly recreational.

From the early 1940s through 1967 there were a number of Canadian municipal or provincial groups involved in wheelchair basketball. Bill Hepburn of the Montreal Wheelchair Wonders and Stan Stronge of the Vancouver Dueck Powerglides were among the most notable individuals involved in the sport. The Montreal team represented Canada in the Stoke Mandeville Wheelchair Games in 1953, marking our nation's start in world competition; this team also represented Canada in 1954 at the sixth National Wheelchair

Basketball Tournament in New York.

During the 1960s familiar names in the sport included Smithson, Knightingale, Coates, Bagnatto, Wendel, Fertile, Warrior and Marshall. Al Simpson of Winnipeg, Manitoba, recalls an event organized in Saskatoon in 1963, which he claims may have represented the first interprovincial basketball competition: teams from Winnipeg and Edmonton met in Saskatoon to participate in a weekend of basketball. In 1967, Simpson became the managing director of the Pan American Games for the Disabled, which were held in Winnipeg in August of that year. He recalls that the operating budget for that event was $17,148 and that there were a total of 128 athletes from five nations represented. Organizational discussions for the Canadian Wheelchair Sports Association (CWSA) took place during this event and on September 9, 1967, the CWSA was born. Dr. Robert W. Jackson was elected chair.

Canada's Tracey Ferguson throws the basketball.

From 1968 through 1978, the national championships for wheelchair basketball were held in conjunction with all other wheelchair sport championship events. In 1979, basketball was organized as an event separate from the rest of wheelchair sports, and the provincial teams competed for the Maxine K. Cooper memorial trophy. That award was retired in 1986 and the teams now compete for the Robert W. Jackson trophy. Over the years there has been active competition between the provinces. British Columbia has won 13 national championships, Alberta 8, Nova Scotia 1 and Ontario 6. British Columbia won consecutively from 1978 through 1983. Alberta had consecutive wins from 1984 through 1990, giving it the distinction of having dominated the sport for seven years — a record in Canada.

In 1986, the Canadian Wheelchair Basketball League (CWBL) was founded. Club teams compete for the national title using a 15-point classification system (with able-bodied athletes classified as 4.5). In 1990, the CWBL women's conference combined their finals with the national championships. They named their trophy in honour of longtime supporter Dr. Donald Royer. Finally, recognizing a need to provide a national event for juniors, the Canadian Wheelchair Basketball Association (CWBA) introduced the Junior and Mini Basket CWBL Finals in 1994.

In addition to national competitions, teams have been selected to represent Canada at numerous international meets over the years. The first team to be selected went to the Paralympics in Israel in 1968. (Paralympic games were now organized away from Stoke Mandeville.) The games in Israel, like those which had taken place in Rome in 1960 and in Tokyo in 1964, featured outdoor courts.

Today there are over 2000 athletes competing in various city leagues, the CWBL (50 teams for men, women and youth) and the National Wheelchair Basketball Association (165 teams for men, women, youth and collegiate players in North America). With the formation of the CWBA, the future is bright for wheelchair basketball in Canada. The people involved in wheelchair basketball in the early days paved the way for modern-day athletes. As a result of their work, there are many opportunities available to today's athletes. The Canada Games Council recognized the sport for the first time at the 1995 Canada Games in Alberta. Also in 1995, Sport Canada recognized CWBA athletes by providing them "carding" status, which means that approximately $250,000 is available annually to contribute to the sport's development. In 1996, 12 men's teams and eight women's teams competed in the tenth Paralympic Games in Atlanta. As a result of the efforts and incredible commitment of athletes, coaches, officials and administrators over the years, the general public is more aware than ever of the positive contributions made by wheelchair athletes on and off the basketball court.

Athletes with paraplegia, cerebral palsy (CP) and amputations, as well as those classified as les autres (LA) compete in wheelchair basketball. With minimal rule modifications, the game is virtually the same as that played in the Olympic Games. Games last for 50 minutes (two 20-minute periods with a 10-minute half time). The wheelchair is considered part of the body when interpreting contact on the floor. Athletes may take two pushes and then pass, dribble or shoot the ball. No double dribble rule applies, but a third push is considered travelling. When taking foul shots or three-point shots, the shooter's rear wheels must be behind the foul line or the three-point line. A technical foul is called if a player puts his or her feet on the floor or rises out of the chair.

■ SPORT HIGHLIGHTS

Canada's men's team won a silver medal at the 1986 Gold Cup World Championships in Melbourne, Australia, and struck gold in international competition in 1989 at the Stoke Mandeville Wheelchair Games. In 1990, both men's and women'd teams finished with bronze medals at their respective gold cups, and both captured gold at the 1991 Stoke Mandeville Wheelchair Games. The men finished fourth at the Paralympics in Barcelona, Spain, in 1992, while the women captured the first gold medal for Canada at that event. In 1994, the women repeated their gold medal performance at the World Championships while the men settled for bronze at their Gold Cup World Championship. That event was hosted by Canada in Edmonton, AB. In 1996, the Canadian women's national team won a gold medal at the Paralympics in Atlanta.

ATHLETE PROFILE

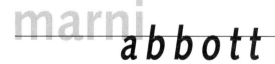

marni **abbott**

Key Event: Wheelchair Basketball

Card: A

Category: IV

Birthdate: 10/11/1965

Birthplace: Nelson, BC

Current Residence: Vancouver, BC

■ CAREER HIGHLIGHT

Gold medal winner at the 1992 Barcelona Paralympics and 1996 Atlanta Paralympics in wheelchair basketball

Marlene (Marni) Marie Abbott spent her early years near Enderby, BC, until the accident that put her in a wheelchair, which occurred in 1983 while she was skiing.

Shayna Hornstein, the physiotherapist at Shaughnessy Hospital where Marni was taken after the accident, had Marni up and swimming in the pool about three weeks after the accident. Shayna introduced Marni to wheelchair sports while Marni was still bedridden, in part by regaling Marni with stories about a recent trip to France with the National Wheelchair Basketball Team. Shayna is the person Marni credits the most for what she has accomplished today. Shayna's support and encouragement gave Marni the tools she needed to carry on her life as a disabled women and to pursue her dreams.

In addition to basketball, Marni swims and plays water sports. Her family has a cottage on Okanagan Lake, so much of her spare time is spent there. "We do a lot of camping, fishing, kayaking and waterskiing," says Marni. Over the years she has tried most sports: tennis, volleyball (she currently plays in an able-bodied grass league with her friends), hockey (sledge hockey and ball hockey, although "the guys always stick me in goal," laughs Marnie), sitskiing and bungie jumping, which Marni highly recommends.

"Finally, there's some equality in this sport! It has taken a long time, and there's still a long way to go, but things are moving forward."

The accomplishment in which Marni takes the most pride is her participation on one of the most outstanding women's wheelchair basketball teams in history — the team that won the gold medal at the 1992 Barcelona Paralympics. Winning the gold was an incredible experience, remembers Marni. As a rookie on the team, she was overwhelmed by the victory. Winning another gold at the 1996 Atlanta Paralympics was just as precious because this time her parents (along with many of Marni's teammates' families) were there to share in the glory. Marni was the Canadian team's flagbearer at the opening ceremonies in Atlanta — a very special honour.

Marni says, "This team just keeps getting better, and we will continue to amaze the world as we go for our third straight Paralympic gold in 2000 in Sydney. We're just gearing up now for the world championships [the Gold Cup] in Australia this fall. This will be the first time the men's and women's Gold Cup will be held in the same place at the same time … Finally, there's some equality in this sport! It has taken a long time, and there's still a long way to go, but things are moving forward. It's a good thing for us girls!"

Marni's biggest disappointment is that, despite the great success of the team internationally, Marni and her teammates have not been able to win the Canadian National Championships. This is a personal disappointment for Marni because she was involved in founding the team and naming it the "BC Breakers" in 1991. Since its inception, the team has had great success in development, coaching and recruiting, and has sent many girls through its program. The Breakers have made it to the finals four times but have always placed second or third — one year they lost the championship by one point. Says Marni, "The funny thing is, the teams that have ended up beating us in the championships

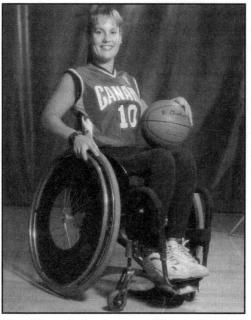

Marni Abbott in the Canadian National Team uniform, 1996.

are teams we've beat during the season. We know we are the best team in the country, we just don't have the hardware to prove it!"

The BC Breakers is composed largely of able-bodied women who put in time, effort and dedication. If it wasn't for their involvement, Marni notes, she and other players with a disability would not have a women's team to play on or practice with during the year. Many other players on the national team are in the same situation — they have recruited many able-bodied players across Canada to play on the league teams and this has improved the league immensely. Marni credits the strength of the national team in women's wheelchair basketball to the quality of the leagues in Canada. So far, Canada is the only country in the world to involve able-bodied athletes in wheelchair basketball.

In looking to the future, Marni comments, "I see only good things for the sport of wheelchair basketball — good things for both men and women. We recently received carding status from the federal government, and this has helped improve training and travel opportunities for athletes. Right now, though, there are some problems as there are some positions open on our board and we don't really have anyone stepping into these positions with the experience and knowledge required to do a good job. One of the most significant barriers to the progress of wheelchair basketball is lack of media coverage and lack of funding for both athletes and coaches. Although the carding money helps, we need some huge corporate sponsorship to really take our leagues into the future."

For the last two years Marni has been playing on a team in the USA national wheelchair basketball league as well as on the BC team. Marni and some women from Oregon, Washington and Alberta have formed a regional team. Their first year in the league they earned second place in the nationals, and in March 1997 in Minneapolis they won the national NWBA championship. Marni states, "It was very exciting! It was weird to be named first tournament All-American though!" The game was televised in June 1997 on ESPN.

For the last six years Marni has been a member of the BC Wheelchair Sports Demo Team, which travels to schools throughout BC, sharing important messages regarding safety, injury prevention, PMA (positive mental attitude) and reverse integration. Among other benefits, playing basketball has given Marni a vehicle to help educate youth and create awareness throughout society. She says she can't imagine her life without wheelchair basketball and disabled sport opportunities. The sport has allowed her to stay physically fit and healthy, and she also has a great time training hard and working toward mutual goals with other committed people. Meeting and surpassing those goals is just the "icing on the cake."

ATHLETE PROFILE

elaine *ell*

Key Event: Wheelchair basketball

Card: uncarded

Classification: 4 ISMWSF

Birthdate: 1938

Birthplace: Grassy Lake, AB

Current Residence: Edmonton, AB

■ CAREER HIGHLIGHTS

Played wheelchair basketball in the 1976, 1980 and 1988 Paralympics; inducted into the Alberta Sports Hall of Fame in 1976

The longevity of any athletic career is determined by a number of factors. Among the attributes that help, patience is probably the most valuable to an athlete hoping to have a long and prosperous career in sport. Alberta's Elaine Ell is a living testament to both patience and athletic skill.

From 1959 to 1967, Elaine was one of Canada's top female all-round wheelchair athletes. In 1967 she attended the very first National Wheelchair Championship in Montreal and witnessed the founding of the Canadian Wheelchair Sports Association (CWSA) shortly thereafter. In 1969, Elaine attended the Pan American Wheelchair Games in Argentina. And for 20 years, from 1969 to 1988, she represented Team Alberta in one sport or another at the Canadian Wheelchair Games.

In the early days, injury often played a significant role in athletic performance, especially given the number of events in which the athletes had to compete. "It was not unheard of to compete in 8 to 12 events in the early days," explains Elaine. "When we were in so many events, it actually was harmful to us, including myself, who had injuries. Yet we kept playing through those injuries. We didn't have access to good training facilities and medical knowledge." Although the athletic intensity and pressure was not as severe as it is today, there was stress of a different kind. Elaine often had to compete in events when she would have preferred not to. "At the Pan Ams in Mexico I had to compete in Dartchery with Brian Ward as a partner," she remembers. "It all came down to my final throw to win the gold medal. I made the throw and Brian and I won the gold. I was the most surprised athlete there!"

After the 1976 Paralympics, Elaine began to specialize in the sport of wheelchair basketball. "I was rarely a starter on the national team, and in some games I didn't get very much floor time, but I hung in there for 20 years, which left me with a good feeling," she says.

It was also at that time Elaine began to develop her professional career as a sport administrator. The leap from athlete to administrator was not a completely unfamiliar one. "Even as an athlete I wore two hats as an athlete and a volunteer administrator," she says. "I served as president of the Paralympic Sports Club as well as their executive director." Elaine's timing was right too. "The whole development of sport for people with disabilities has reflected a change in society's attitude toward people with disabilities," explains Elaine. "We could never have started as part of the non-disabled sport groups. We needed our own NSOs [national sports organizations] to lobby on our behalf, to fight for us and give us the things we have today."

> *"We could never have started as part of the non-disabled sport groups. We needed our own NSOs."*

Proving herself as an administrator turned out to be more difficult than proving her athletic skill on a basketball court. Elaine had spent many of her early years institutionalized in a Calgary children's hospital without the opportunity to mature in the same way as other children, socially or academically. After working as a sports administrator for the Alberta government for 17 years, Elaine gained skills that she had been denied the opportunity to develop previously.

When Elaine moved on to a position as the assistant public relations director for the Edmonton Oilers, she got to see sports organizations from a different vantage point. Her nine-year stint watching the hockey club develop into Stanley Cup champions had a considerable influence on Elaine's subsequent involvement in disability sports administration. Elaine's career as a disability sports administrator began when she left the Oilers for a position with Edmonton's Paralympic Sports Club. This wheelchair sports organization administered all sports except basketball for wheelchair athletes in the city. Five years later, Elaine moved on to her favourite sport, accepting a position with the Alberta Northern Lights basketball team.

Elaine maintains she perceived very few barriers in her careers as athlete and administrator. "If you are qualified to do the job you should be given every opportunity to give it a try," she says. "Hiring someone just because the person has a disability can lead to problems. That person must recognize the amount of responsibility in any position and combine that with academic skills. If you don't have those skills, your job will become a very difficult one."

Today, even though she is retired from her position with the Alberta Northern Lights, Elaine continues to be involved with the Alberta Wheelchair Sports Association and will be running for president at the next annual general meeting. In her own words: "Being involved in wheelchair sports has really provided me with a wealth of experience and developed my self-confidence for everyday living. I'm very grateful for what it provided me."

Elaine Ell (with ball) and teammates in 1988.

WHEELCHAIR RUGBY

Wheelchair rugby was invented in 1978 by five Canadians from Winnipeg, Manitoba. The sport quickly gained acceptance and provincial teams were formed. The first exhibition game was held in 1979 at a regional track meet in Marshall, Minnesota. Canada went on to host its first national championship that same year.

In 1988 the University of North Dakota hosted the first International Wheelchair Rugby Tournament; teams from Manitoba, Saskatchewan, North Dakota and Minnesota participated. Today, over 15 countries on four continents compete in wheelchair rugby. Furthermore, rugby is officially recognized by the International Stoke Mandeville Wheelchair Sports Federation, the world governing body for wheelchair sport. In North America alone there are over 50 club teams. A minimum of 10 national and international tournaments are hosted each year.

Wheelchair rugby is a very fast, contact game played between two teams of four players.

Wheelchair rugby is a very fast, contact game played between two teams of four players. It combines elements of basketball, football and ice hockey. Players carry, dribble, throw or pass a volleyball while moving toward the opponent's goal area. The team with the greatest point total upon completion of the game is declared the winner.

The rugby playing court has the same dimensions as a regulation basketball court (26 metres long by14 metres wide). The goal is identified by two cone-shaped standards placed eight metres apart. The key area, in which only three defensive players may reside

Competitiors in the Wheelchair Rugby National Championships.

at one time, is 1.75 metres in depth. A regulation volleyball is played with the hands or forearms, or carried on the player's lap. The player must dribble or pass the ball at least once every 10 seconds. A goal is scored when a player in control of the ball touches the goal line with two wheels. Rugby is played in four eight-minute quarters. Game violations include spinning, charging and interference.

All wheelchair rugby athletes must be classified as quadriplegics. This classification most often arises from an injury to the cervical level of the spinal cord. Such trauma results in varying degrees of paralysis to the legs, trunk and arms. As a result, different players have different levels of physical ability. Because not all players have similar levels of ability, players must be classified by a certified classification expert. All players receive a classification between 0.5 and 3.5 points. To ensure fair and competitive play, the total combined point value of a team's players on the floor may not exceed eight. All games are officiated by two experienced referees. Other support staff include a timekeeper, a penalty timekeeper and a scorer.

■ SPORT HIGHLIGHT

Canada achieved second place at the first World Wheelchair Rugby Championship in 1995.

WHEELCHAIR TENNIS

Combining skill, fitness and strategy, wheelchair tennis is one of the fastest-growing sports for athletes with a disability. It is unique in the sports world since an able-bodied player can compete with a person who uses a wheelchair and the two players will be relatively equally matched.

The sport rapidly became one of the fastest-growing and most challenging of all wheelchair sports.

Wheelchair tennis originated in the United States in 1976 when the first wheelchair tennis tournament was held in Los Angeles, California. In 1980, the National Foundation of Wheelchair Tennis was established in the United States and the sport rapidly became one of the fastest-growing and most challenging of all wheelchair sports both in the US and internationally. The International Wheelchair Tennis Federation (IWTF) was founded in 1988 with eight member nations, including Canada. In 1991 the IWTF was absorbed by the International Tennis Federation (ITF), underlining the federation's commitment to the sport at the highest level among wheelchair athletes. Today, the IWTF branch of the ITF has 48 member nations.

Wheelchair tennis became an official Paralympic Games sport at the Barcelona Games in 1992. At those games, 48 players — 32 men and 16 women —from 16 international delegations took part in the singles and doubles competitions. In addition to the Paralympics, wheelchair tennis athletes may compete in many events and tournaments around the world. At the end of each calendar year, the IWTF considers NEC Wheelchair Tennis Rankings, National Rankings and other relevant information to determine recipients of World Champion Awards.

An athlete desiring to play wheelchair tennis must be medically diagnosed as having a mobility-related disability that required the use of a wheelchair. One classification accommodates all players. Wheelchair tennis is played on a regulation tennis court and follows traditional tennis rules, maintaining the same tradition of high levels of skill, fitness and strategy. The only difference in wheelchair tennis competitions is that the players are allowed two bounces of the ball, the first bounce being within the bounds of the court. Singles and doubles events are included in the Paralympic program.

The equipment used by wheelchair-tennis athletes is basically the same as that used by able-bodied tennis players — with the obvious exception of the wheelchair. These chairs differ considerably from chairs used in other disabled sports. They are designed for quick changes of direction and allow the athlete to swing a racket easily. Athletes may use straps to secure themselves to their wheelchairs and some athletes use devices to help them hold the racket.

Three of the most important events in wheelchair tennis are the Action World Team Cup, the NEC International Wheelchair Tennis Tour and the Paralympics. Here are some highlights in the history of each of these competitions:

Action World Team Cup

1985: The World Team Cup is the official team event of the IWTF for both men and women. World Team Cup players have the opportunity to represent their countries in an international competition comparable to the Davis Cup in able-bodied tennis. Athletes from six countries entered the first World Team Cup.

1995: Within 10 years of its inception, there were 29 men's teams and 16 women's teams competing in the World Team Cup.

1996: Action, the wheelchair producer and division of Invacare, became the title sponsor of the World Team Cup. In the men's competition, Australia defeated France while in the women's event, the Netherlands defeated the United States.

NEC International Wheelchair Tennis Tour and Ranking

1992: Supported by NEC, the IWTF formalized the NEC International Wheelchair Tennis Tour. Players who compete in the top divisions of any IWTF sanctioned event receive points on the NEC ranking system. The six best results for each man, and the five best for each woman, are combined to establish a player's overall ranking.

The most prestigious event on the Tour — the NEC Wheelchair Tennis Masters — was also established in 1992. The leading eight men and women are invited to compete in the elite tournament at the end of each year in Eindhoven, the Netherlands.

1998: The NEC International Wheelchair Tennis Tour now consists of over a hundred tournaments, including Satellites, the Championship Series and, of course, the US Open and the British Open.

Paralympics

1992, Barcelona: Wheelchair tennis became a fully accredited medal sport and the event attracts 48 athletes from 16 nations.

1996, Atlanta: A total of 72 athletes from 24 nations participated in the wheelchair tennis events at the Paralympics in Atlanta, illustrating the dramatic development of the sport in recent years.

■ SPORT HIGHLIGHTS

Mario Perron, Paul Johnson and Daniel Wesley are Canada's top tennis players. Perron, who comes from Brossard, QC, finished in second place at the 1996 World Cup.

ATHLETE PROFILE

paul *johnson*

Key Event: Wheelchair tennis

Birthdate: 10/09/66

Birthplace: Albert Bay, BC

Residence: Victoria, BC

Club: Oak Bay Recreation Centre

Coach: Eric Knoester

Paul Johnson was the Canadian Singles Champion for five consecutive years, from 1991 to 1995. He was also a member of the Canadian Doubles Championship Team from 1993 to 1995. He has been a member of the national team for nine years.

Paul was introduced to the sport of wheelchair tennis through his rehabilitation program over 10 years ago. A leader in the sport, Paul hopes his involvement and high world ranking will encourage more people to become involved in the sport. Among the accomplishments that give him the most satisfaction are his status as the Canadian Singles Champion, competing in the Paralympics in Barcelona in 1992 and making it to the finals at the Swedish Open the same year. Paul's greatest memory since becoming involved in wheelchair tennis was playing American tennis great Randy Snow at the World Team Cup in Irvine, California in 1991.

Paul enjoys the camaraderie between the players from different countries when he competes. When not competing, Paul can usually be found fishing or weight training. He is also a dog lover and feels that his dog forces him to be responsible — preparing him for the greater responsibility of a family in the future.

■ Competition History Highlights

1996: World Team Cup Team — 10th
1995: Canadian Championships Singles — 1st
1995: Canadian Championships Doubles — 1st
1995: World Team Cup Team — 13th
1994: Canadian Championships Singles — 1st

2

The Organizations
and the Organizers

CANADIAN AMPUTEE SPORTS ASSOCIATION

CASA

A Brief History

Amputees have long been at the forefront of the disability sport movement internationally and in Canada. In the United States and Great Britain, national golf associations for amputees have been in existence since the end of the Second World War. In Canada, amputees have participated in many sports — skiing and wheelchair basketball, in particular — since the early 1950s. The development of three-track skiing enabled above- and below-knee amputees to ski the slopes at Banff and Jasper in the early 1960s. The amendments to wheelchair basketball rules that allow amputees to compete have encouraged many amputees to take up this sport.

It was not until 1976, however, when the Canadian Amputee Sports Association (CASA) was formed, that Canadian amputees had a unified organization in sport. As with a number of other disability sport groups in Canada, CASA got its start as a result of funding re-directed from the ill-fated 1976 Toronto Paralympiad (which was boycotted because of the presence of South African athletes).

CASA's first president, John Gibson, was an elderly, outgoing gentleman who was an avid photographer. John Gibson steered CASA through its formative years. In 1980 he was replaced as president by Gerry Sorenson, a double below-knee amputee from Newfoundland, who in turn was replaced a year later by Alan Dean, a below-knee amputee from Aurora, Ontario, and a former athlete. Alan Dean held the president's position from 1982 until 1992, when he was succeeded by Calgary athlete Patrick Jarvis. When Pat Jarvis retired in 1994, he was replaced by longtime volunteer and retired oil company worker Bob Wade. Bob is the first non-amputee to preside over CASA since John Gibson, 20 years before.

CASA has traditionally had representation from all provinces, including Quebec. For the first decade of its existence, CASA maintained a high number of athletes in its membership and an exceptionally high medal return from its athletes. This was due, in part, to the fact that in the early days it was not uncommon for one athlete to compete in a variety of different sports. Athletes such as long-jump world record holder Arnie Boldt played volleyball as well as competing in track and field events. It was not uncommon to see powerlifters and swimmers playing volleyball as well.

Toward the end of the 1980s, CASA weathered a gradual decline in the number of its athletes, although the overall calibre of the athletes increased. In 1984, for example, at the International Games for the Disabled in New York, CASA fielded a team of over 40 athletes and staff. In 1996 at the Atlanta Paralympics, only 10 amputees represented Canada in five sports: powerlifting (2), athletics (3), swimming (2), shooting (1), sailing (1) and cycling (1). The general movement within disability sports organizations toward a sport-specific (instead of disability-specific) focus may have had a detrimental effect on the number of CASA athletes who attended the Paralympics. There also has been a trend to support non-Paralympic sports, such as golf, within CASA.

One of the problems facing CASA has been the inability to dedicate funding for an essential Ottawa-based staffperson. While this national sports organization did have one part-time employee in the mid-1980s, funding for the position was redirected when federal cutbacks took place in the 1990s. There is no doubt that if CASA could have maintained a nationally based staffperson it would been more successful in weathering many of the problems it faced in the 1990s.

In recent years CASA had the opportunity to bolster its ranks considerably by choosing to incorporate the Les Autres (LA) category. (The LA category includes all physical disabilities not included under "spinal injured" and "cerebral palsy.") However, resistance within CASA squelched this excellent growth opportunity. Including the LA category would no doubt have necessitated a name change for the organization, and CASA seemed unwilling to make such a drastic move. As it stands today, the LA category of athlete spans membership in CASA and the Canadian Cerebral Palsy Sports Association (CCPSA).

CASA's inability to change in accordance with developments at the international level has once again left Canada's amputees to fend for

Ian Gregson and Claude Poumerol at the 1985 Canadian Games.

themselves — something that, fortunately, they are good at. Nonetheless, it is unfortunate that while other NSOs representing athletes with disabilities have been able to work through inevitable changes, CASA remains locked in a 1970s mode of thought. Talks of amalgamation with the Canadian Wheelchair Sports Association (CWSA) and the CCPSA have lead to naught.

CASA has clearly suffered from a lack of new vision. The inability of CASA's national executive to communicate effectively with the average active amputee living in Canada, as well as with other like-minded organizations, is indicative of the internal problems facing this organization. Unless drastic changes are made within CASA, it is liable to lose federal funding in the near future — and we will be left without an organized national amputee sport program in Canada.

Author's Note: Since this chapter was written, CASA has lost all federal funding.

norma suarez-jordan

Key Events: Discus, Shot-put

Qualification: Level III NCCP

Birthdate: 20/01/1940

Birthplace: Argentina

Current Residence: Richmond, BC

Coach: Athletics (Field Events)

CAREER HIGHLIGHT

Coach at Paralympic Games in 1988, 1992 and 1996

It is rare for a disability sports organization to have the honour of a former Olympic athlete in its coaching ranks. For CASA and amputee athletes, one such honour appears in the person of Richmond, BC's Norma Suarez-Jordan, a veteran of the 1964 and 1968 Olympic Games in the discus and shot-put.

Norma was introduced to disability sport in 1986, through an unfortunate circumstance at a track meet in Langley, BC. The author, Paralympian Ian Gregson, had sprained his ankle in a warm-up for the discus event. The pain was so intense that Ian passed out and collapsed. When he awoke he was face-to-face with Norma Jordan, and from that point on, Norma became Ian's coach in the discus event. She subsequently went on to coach numerous top-level athletes with a disability in the discus and shot-put.

She quickly found out that none of the support mechanisms that existed for her non-disabled athletes were in place for athletes with a disability

Norma's exposure to the world of disability sport gave her some sharp shocks. She quickly found that none of the support mechanisms that existed for her non-disabled athletes were in place for athletes with a disability. Even though many of her athletes with a disability had placed within the top five at international events, federal "carding" was unavailable to them (non-disabled elite athletes were given "carded" status, which allowed them access to federal funding while training). This situation led to many board-level battles with CASA.

Despite ongoing setbacks with funding, Norma persevered, taking the skills she had honed with both Athletics Canada and her involvement in Canadian disability sport and combining them into one unique and rare talent. She now coaches Canada's top blind thrower and world record holder Ljiljana Ljubisic. Norma Suarez-Jordan stands out as a perfect example of how top coaching talent can be equally beneficial, and essential, to athletes with and without a disability.

CANADIAN ASSOCIATION OF DISABLED SKIERS
CADS

A Brief History

The history of skiing for people with disabilities in Canada is synonymous with Jerry Johnston and his wife Ann. From the early 1960s on, Jerry and Ann have developed their ski program for people with disabilities into a national association and have sent many medal-winning athletes to Paralympic and World Championship events.

It all began in 1963, when Jerry was teaching at the Sunshine Ski School in Banff, Alberta. He was asked to teach a young girl who had had polio how to ski. That process took almost 14 days, and it marked the first time a person with a disability had been taught to ski. Today, the same instruction would take about four hours.

The first formal recognition of skiers with disabilities occurred in 1968, when there was a demonstration involving disabled skiers at an Interski meeting in Colorado, USA. Over Christmas

A CADS magazine cover from the 1970s.

1969, Jerry Johnston invited several top American skiers, including Hal O'Leary, Jim Witters and Dan McPherson from California, to work on the development of a Canadian-based organization for skiers with a disability. In 1970, Sue Clift, with the assistance of the Canadian Ski Instructors Alliance, wrote the first manual on teaching people with disabilities how to ski. And in 1971 the first provincial organization — the Alberta Disabled Skiers Association — was formed.

Government funding proved instrumental in the formation of a national organization. In 1975 funds were diverted from the Toronto Paralympiad (because of a boycott of the games due to the participation of South Africa), and the Canadian Association of Disabled Skiers (CADS) was officially formed.

CADS Today

In the late 1990s, governments are not so generous with the tax dollars as they were in the mid-1970s. Jerry Johnston comments, "With the economy the way it is and all the cutbacks, our situation [at CADS] is not likely to improve. But there is still some core funding there. They always throw some money into the summer and winter Paralympics. We've received some extra funding to prepare the team to go to Japan in 1998. But I don't think the money will be there after 1998." Currently, three of Canada's top skiers with disabilities receive funds through the Federal Athlete Assistance program (a program that provides assistance to elite non-disabled and disabled athletes).

One of CADS' accomplishments was to support the 1980 initiative that allowed amputee skiers to have the option of using outriggers or poles. CADS also supported the inclusion of skiers with other disabilities, such as post-polio athletes or those with cerebral palsy, into a combined "functional" classification system. Prior to 1980, only amputees who had lost limbs through traumatic circumstances (accidents and other traumatic events) were allowed to compete as skiers. The CADS organization was also a model for other nations and was closely involved in initiating the disabled skiing program in Japan.

ORGANIZER PROFILE

jerry johnston

Years of Involvement: 1962 to present

■ CAREER HIGHLIGHT

With spouse Ann Johnston, developed a ski program for people with disabilities into a national association and sent many athletes to Paralympic and World Championship events.

Johnston's Thoughts on CADS

Although he has had many successes with CADS, one of Jerry Johnston's biggest disappointments has been the organization's failure to receive the co-operation of other like-minded disability groups such as the War Amps of Canada. "They have a large number of amputee kids in their CHAMPS program, but our relationship has been tentative at best. Although we do have some of our kids in their program, we can't seem to combine the programs."

"...we are getting off the sympathy page and into the sports section."

Johnston also cites a lack of media attention for CADS as a major disappointment although, he observes, "recently we are getting off the sympathy page and into the sports section a little more."

Johnston and his dedicated team of vounteers have worked hard to raise the corporate profile of CADS. "Some corporations get involved and stay for a few years," he says. "The longest corporate sponsor we had was the Canadian Imperial Bank of Commerce, and they were involved for six-and-a-half years. Shell and the RJR Tobacco company have also been involved over the years. We are always looking for corporate sponsorship."

Johnston also sees the issue of allocation of funds from the international disability sports body — the International Paralympic Committee (IPC) — as a major source of headache and concern. "The politics of the International Paralympic Committee are somewhat dollar consuming. The winter technical committee only gets $9000 a year for meetings, whereas the treasurer of the IPC spends that himself."

According to Johnston, the dynamics of recreation and sport are forever changing and the effects of these changes on CADS are obvious. "CADS will continue to grow. We have more people every year. But we are not getting the same number of competitors — people just don't seem to have the free time anymore."

The movement toward inclusion has had limited success across Canada in the sport of skiing. Nonetheless, several CADS athletes compete in non-disabled Alpine Canada events. According to Johnston, "We are fitting into the able-bodied system to some degree. Although it [integration] sounds good in theory, the problem is it works in Alberta because there are only five or six skiers who compete in the races. When you go to Southern Ontario you have 180 able-bodied kids, and you can't just add half a dozen kids with disabilities to the race. So in certain areas of the country it will work but in others it won't. The logistics are stopping the move towards total integration. Using the same coaches and the same officials [as able-bodied skiers] is a great idea, and we are doing what we can, but integration is not the solution to all our problems."

Canada maintains one of the healthiest ski programs for people with disabilities in the world today

Jerry Johnston was instrumental in forming the Canadian Federation of Sports Organizations for the Disabled (CFSOD) and, later on, the Canadian Paralympic Committee (CPC). When the Canadian Wheelchair Sports Association (CWSA) pulled out of the CPC and everyone thought it was going to die, Johnston, along with Gerry York of the Canadian Blind Sports Association (CBSA) and members of the Canadian Amputee Sports Association (CASA), were instrumental in keeping the CPC alive.

Even with government cutbacks, lack of solid media recognition and lack of co-operation from like-minded groups, Canada maintains one of the healthiest ski programs for people with disabilities in the world today. This is a testament to Jerry Johnston's commitment and work — as are the medals that Canadian skiers with a disability consistently win at international competitions like the Paralympics.

CANADIAN BLIND SPORTS ASSOCIATION
CBSA

A Brief History

Like the Canadian Amputee Sports Association (CASA) and the Canadian Association of Disabled Skiers (CADS), the Canadian Blind Sports Association (CBSA) found itself on the receiving end of funds diverted from the 1976 Toronto Paralympiad. As was the case with many of its fellow disability sports organizations, the CBSA had already developed provincially in British Columbia, Ontario and Alberta prior to the formation of the national association in 1976.

Since 1976 the Canadian Blind Sports Association has fielded teams for various international events such as the Paralympics and World Championships. Canadian blind and partially sighted athletes have gained respect throughout the world as top-quality high performance athletes.

Courtney Knight of the CBSA tosses a ball with a young friend.

Blind swimmer being "tapped."

ORGANIZER PROFILE

gerry *york*

Birthdate: 1920

Birthplace: Winnipeg, MB

Current Residence: Vancouver, BC

Years of Involvement: 1976 to present

■ CAREER HIGHLIGHT

President of CBSA from 1980 to 1984; heavily involved in the beginnings of the Canadian Federation of Sports Organizations for the Disabled (CFSOD)

Following is an interview conducted by the author with Gerry York.

Why did you become involved with sports for the blind?
My son Patrick is blind.

When did you first become involved?
I was involved in sport to begin with because of my other children. My daughter Terrie was an Olympic class diver and I was already involved with the Canadian Amateur Diving Association when the 1976 Toronto Paralympiad came along. That is when people started talking about having Olympics for the disabled. Because I was already involved in sport, I made some enquiries as to the opportunities for blind athletes if the Paralympics were going to happen. Joe Louis at the Canadian National Institute for the Blind (CNIB) was very helpful and I basically started out by helping as a parent.

After 1976 the federal government showed support for the formation of national associations for disabled athletes. The province of Ontario was active in all our sport organizations, and we all have similar beginnings.

How did you get involved as a board member of the CBSA?

I sort of became president by default in 1980. I was the treasurer previously. I was invited to a symposium in late 1979. Dick Loiselle, Gordy Cameron and Paul DuPrey were also involved in this symposium.

After this meeting I was invited to be president pro-tem as the president at the time didn't want to complete her full term. I was to be team manager of the Paralympic team for Arnhem in 1980, and in May 1980 I was officially elected. I remained as president from 1980 until 1984. I was heavily involved in the beginnings of the Canadian Federation of Sports Organizations for the Disabled (CFSOD).

After I retired I was encouraged by Merv Oveson to become president of the British Columbia chapter of the CBSA.

"One highlight is whenever an athlete with a disability sets a new standard, whether it be a world record or a personal best."

What are some of the highlights of the last 20 years for you?

There's more than one, but I can put my finger on a few highlights. Overall it is whenever an athlete with a disability sets a new standard, whether it be a world record or a personal best. I can still remember Yvette Michel in 1979 setting a world record in Richmond, BC. We were at the end of a very tiring weekend and all of a sudden the judges were re-checking their watches and no one felt tired anymore.

Another was my son Patrick winning his gold medal at the 1980 Paralympics in Holland. Right at the end of the race, with several other competitors closing in, Patrick broke free of the tether with the guide and ran the last 20 metres by himself. Dick Loiselle caught Pat at the end and told him he had won.

Also, Arnie Boldt in Seoul was another highlight. We had the biggest-ever crowd at the Paralympics. Arnie was trying to break his world record in the high jump and he got very close, and the very large crowd was behind him. I was really moved by the crowd getting behind Arnie since hardly anyone had come out to see him in Holland and in New York.

It is these kind of performances that inspire me to tell young kids in high school (whether they have a disability or not) that they too can strive to go to the Olympics and win a medal. Anyone who claims a personal best makes me glad I volunteered.

And what are some of the disappointments for you in organizing sport for athletes with a disability?

I'm an eternal optimist and I try not to dwell on the negative things. One of the things that does bother me is not being able to get enough competitiors in some of the events, particularly the women's events. This causes the event to be dropped from the Paralympic calendar or the classifications have to be combined. I'm always taking World Health Organization (WHO) figures to the government to tell them, "You can't have the same requirements for federal carding for disabled athletes as for non-disabled athletes." The numbers game is always a problem for blind women athletes. Ljiljana Ljubisic in Atlanta had to compete against B2 athletes, and the B2 throwers threw further than the B3 throwers.

I have not fallen in love with the functional classification system as yet. Partly because I was in Nottingham for the first World Youth Games and saw the devastating effect the functional system was having on some people with disabilities. For instance, kids with above-knee amputations were competing against kids with paralysed lower limbs, and to me that was wrong. I don't care how the classifiers arrived at their mathematical conclusion, the inequity of such a system was more than apparent on that day. We've managed to keep the blind out of functional classification, although I'm sure somebody will dream up a formula to solve that one. Basically, I have a problem with any class system that discriminates in favour of one disability over another. If the playing field cannot be made level, then too bad!

Another issue is more sport based. Blind powerlifters train and compete in all the lifts and yet there is no powerlifting at the Paralympic level for blind athletes. The problem with amputees being banned from able-bodied powerlifting meets is also a problem. The fact that the judges cannot distinguish between an "aid" and something that allows equal access is disturbing.

Having long since "got over" their disability, many disabled athletes today are asking for a better way of measuring their performance. So let's measure their performance in respect to their body mass or some other category — computers can be used for wonderful things these days. We have to motivate the athletes to perform better.

What do you see in the future for disability sport?

In 1994 we had the Commonwealth Games here in Canada and it was a highlight for disability sport across the world as well as in Canada because of the inclusion of athletes with a disability. Then Malaysia was the host of the 1998 Commonwealth Games and we [the athletes with a disability] didn't have any events. Somehow we were so involved in our own worries and with [the Olympics in] Atlanta, we didn't get to the organizers in Malaysia and tell them what we want. Even if it means charging us with an entry fee, money should not be an obstruction to hosting athletes with a disability. I don't want money to ever, ever stop athletes from being able to compete. If it has to be done, put a price on it and let us go out and raise the money somewhere in the world. It's not right that the Commonwealth Games have moved so far ahead — there's planning into the next millennium — and darned if we are not back to square one because of what happened in Malaysia. You think you've won a battle and find out the war is still on.

The work that has been done by organizations and by people like Rick Hansen, and the accomplishments of wheelchair athletes at the Olympics, is something to be further developed. The appearance of wheelchair athletes at the Olympics since 1984 has been an incredible boon for all disability sport. If we fight amongst ourselves over who should be doing what in the Olympics, the International Olympic Committee (IOC) will pick up on that and use it against us. We have to be supportive of each other in principle. We may not agree all the time, but if one disability-based sport group moves ahead then maybe the other groups can benefit also.

"...money should not be an obstruction to hosting athletes with a disability. I don't want money to ever, ever stop athletes from being able to compete."

I'm not in favour of a duplicate delivery system for blind athletes. Our athletes are not physically disabled; they just can't see. So if the necessity for sight is removed, blind athletes should be able to perform as well as sighted athletes. But we have to do this from the day the kid loses his or her sight so that the same motor skills are developed. The only sport that I can see as being fully integrated right now is tandem cycling. In tandem cycling, the person on the back can't see anyway. Swimming would work only if you had good tappers (people who "tap" the swimmers to direct them). This will take time and it would be wonderful not to have a duplicate delivery system — I'd love for our swimmers to have access to nothing but the best coaches. Each disability is different and I don't feel I can speak on behalf of any other disability group. Some disability sports have proven they can compete equally against their non-disabled counterparts when given the chance. But this has to be done on a sport-by-sport basis and it cannot be legislated by the government. I'm scared that Sport Canada will come along and say "thou shalt" ... and then we are dead in the water. It [integration] will only work if the people who are providing the services want it to work.

CANADIAN CEREBRAL PALSY SPORTS ASSOCIATION
CCPSA

(from the CCPSA website)

The Canadian Cerebral Palsy Sports Association (CCPSA) is an athlete-centred national sport organization that encourages and promotes excellence in sports. The CCPSA is a member organization of the Canadian Paralympic Committee (CPC) and the Cerebral Palsy International Sports and Recreation Association. The CCPSA is also recognized by Sport Canada and the Ministry of Canadian Heritage.

Canadian team at the Robin Hood International Games for CP, in Nottingham, England, 1989.

The CCPSA works in partnership with its provincial members to facilitate and promote public awareness of programs. They strive to ensure that athletes have access to, and are encouraged to participate in, competitions and have the opportunity to reach their full athletic potential.

CCPSA athletes are persons with cerebral palsy, head injuries and other related disabilities. These athletes have the opportunity to progress through provincial and national competitions, with the ultimate goal of representing Canada at the Paralympic Games. The Paralympics are the pinnacle of sport for athletes with a disability and are held in the same venues as the Olympic Games (shortly after the Olympics conclude) on the same four-year cycle. CCPSA athletes are dedicated to their respective sports and are supported by their coaches, CCPSA staff and caregivers. The CCPSA is working towards providing opportunities for athletes to be integrated into able-bodied events where possible.

VOLUNTEER PROFILE

faye blackwood

Qualification: Level III NCCP   **Coach:** Athletics (Track Events)

Birthdate: 19/01/57

Birthplace: Toronto, ON

Current Residence: Mississauga, ON

CAREER HIGHLIGHT

Coached all her athletes at the 1992 Paralympics to world records. As an athlete, highlights include: member 1986 Commonwealth Games team in Edinburgh; former Canadian record holder, indoor 60 metre hurdles; 1986 Canadian 100 metre hurdles champion

V eteran coach Faye Blackwood has coached numerous CCPSA athletes — including Ontario's Eric Fleming, Michelle Armstrong and Robert Snoek — to the pinnacle of performance in disability sport.

Blackwood initially became involved in disability sport in 1981 through the Variety Village facility in Toronto. She made the choice to coach athletes with a disability in 1989. This choice was a logical one for Blackwood. "Athletes [with a disability] seem to be much more appreciative and self-confident than their non-disabled counterparts," she states.

"Athletes with a disability seem to be much more appreciative and self-confident than their non-disabled counterparts."

Blackwood's most succesful athlete, Rob Snoek, recently became a B-carded athlete after many years of receiving no direct federal funding. As Blackwood proudly notes, "The carding of athletes [with a disability] has enabled Rob to become a fulltime athlete and his performances this year have been his best."

THE CANADIAN PARALYMPIC COMMITTEE
CPC

(excerpted from the 1996 Canadian Paralympic Team handbook)

I ncorporated in 1994, the Canadian Paralympic Committee (CPC) evolved from the Canadian Federation of Sport Organizations for the Disabled (CFSOD). Recognized by the International Paralympic Committee (IPC), the CPC is responsible for all aspects of Canada's involvement in the Paralympic movement, including Canadian participation in the Paralympic Games.

The CFSOD was at the forefront of a successful lobby for the inclusion of athletes with a disability into major international competitions such as the Olympic and Commonwealth Games. Because the IPC now has the primary responsibility for ongoing lobbying efforts, the focus of the CPC today is Canadian participation in the summer and winter Paralympic Games.

The CPC unites and serves all national member organizations and co-ordinates athletes' participation in the Paralympic Games. Member organizations, and the sports governed by them, include:

Canadian Amputee Sports Association (CASA)

- Athletics
- Cycling
- Powerlifting
- Shooting
- Skiing
- Sledge hockey

Canadian Association for Athletes with a Mental Handicap (CAAMH)

- Athletics

Canadian Blind Sports Association (CBSA)

- Athletics
- Goalball
- Judo
- Lawn bowls
- Skiing

Canadian Cerebral Palsy Sports Association (CCPSA)

- Aathletics
- Boccia
- Ccycling

Canadian Therapeutic Riding Association (CanTRA)

- Equestrian

Canadian Wheelchair Basketball Association (CWBA)

- Basketball

Canadian Wheelchair Sports Association (CWSA)

- Athletics
- Rugby
- Tennis

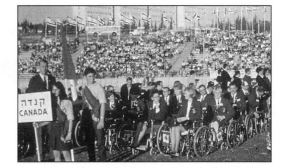

The Canadian Paralympic Team in Tel Aviv, 1968.

Canadian Yachting Association (CYA)

- Yachting

Federation of Canadian Archers (FCA)

- Archery

Shooting Federation of Canada (SFC)

- Shooting

Swimming Natation Canada (SNC)

- Swimming

With the growth of the Paralympic movement, Canada remains a world leader in sport for athletes with a disability. So respected is our country's involvement at the international level that Canadians Dr. Robert Steadward and Dr. Michael Riding hold elected positions with the IPC. Dr. Steadward was elected as the first president of the IPC and was subsequently re-elected to that position in 1993. Dr. Riding is the IPC medical chair.

CPC has undergone operational changes to better serve its member organizations and the athletes they represent. A flexible, responsive team of professional staff and volunteers provide "the best to the best."

ORGANIZER PROFILE

patrick jarvis

Birthdate: 25/08/58

Birthplace: Drumheller, AB

Current Residence: Calgary, AB

■ CAREER HIGHLIGHT

Chef de Mission, 1998 Canadian Winter Paralympic team in Nagano, Japan; CPC Treasurer/Secretary 1993-1996; CPC Vice-President, 1996-98

S ome would say it has been too long coming, but when former Paralympic track-and-field athlete Pat Jarvis was announced as Chef de Mission for the Nagano Paralympics in 1998, a collective shout of "About time!" could be heard from athletes with a disability across the country.

The transition from athlete to volunteer administrator is not easy, and most athletes avoid volunteering for the organizations involved in administering their sport. Still, several athletes with a disability have successfully navigated the transition, and a few became involved in the inaugural "athletes' committee," which was formed in 1991 in an attempt to make Canadian disability sport more athlete centred. In the first few years of its existence the committee had lots of bark and no bite, but has since gone on to develop some influence.

Where most people would lose heart, Patrick Jarvis sees a challenge.

One of the former athletes who took a more direct route towards involvement in administration is Calgary's Patrick Jarvis. After a short and frustrating two-year tenure as president of the Canadian Amputee Sports Association (CASA), in 1993 the amicable Jarvis set his sights on the Canadian Paralympic Committee. At that time, CPC administrators were mostly non-disabled women, many of whom have since moved on to other offices in the National Sport Centre in Ottawa, Ontario. Jarvis broke ground on three fronts: as a man, as a former athlete with a disability and as a western Canadian. This is not unusual for Jarvis: where most people would lose heart, Patrick Jarvis sees a challenge. Perhaps Jarvis' perseverance comes from his stint as the best one-armed bartender in Calgary, or maybe his independence was nurtured through years of being self-employed. Whatever the reasons for his success, Jarvis has the right mix of expertise, diplomacy, patience and all-round amicability to ensure him a bright future with the CPC.

THE CANADIAN SPECIAL OLYMPICS

CndSO

(from the Canadian Special Olympics website)

A Brief History

In the early 1960s, testing of children with cognitive disabilities revealed that they were only half as physically fit as their non-disabled peers. It was assumed that their low fitness levels were a direct result of their disabilities. A Toronto researcher and professor, Dr. Frank Hayden, questioned this assumption. Working with a control group of children on an intense fitness program, he demonstrated that, given the opportunity, mentally handicapped people could become physically fit and acquire the skills necessary to participate in sport. His research proved that low levels of fitness and lack of motor skills development in people with mental handicaps were a result of nothing more than a sedentary life style. In other words, their mental handicaps resulted in their exclusion from the kinds of physical activity and sports experience readily available to other children. Inspired by his discoveries, Dr. Hayden began searching for ways to develop a national sports program for mentally handicapped people. It was a goal he eventually achieved, albeit not in Canada. His work came to the attention of the Kennedy Foundation in Washington, DC, and led to the creation of the Special Olympics. The first sports competitions organized under the Special Olympics banner were held at Soldier Field in Chicago in 1968. To ensure that Canada was represented, Dr. Hayden called on an old friend, Harry "Red" Foster.

The late Red Foster was an outstanding sportsman, a famous broadcaster, a successful businessman and a humanitarian whose tireless work on behalf of people with a mental handicap had already brought him international acclaim. Inspired by his mother's devotion to his younger brother, who was both blind and mentally handicapped, Mr. Foster began early in his career to devote much of his time, energy and wealth to addressing the problems faced by individuals with a mental handicap and by their families. Accompanying a floor hockey team from Toronto to those first games in Chicago, Red was quick to see in Special Olympics a further opportunity to enhance the lives of mentally handicapped Canadians. Upon returning to Canada he set about laying the foundation for the Special Olympics movement. The following summer, 1969, the first Canadian Special Olympics event was held in Toronto. From that modest beginning the Special Olympics movement quickly spread across the country and grew into the national sports organization it is today.

About the Canadian Special Olympics

- The mission of Canadian Special Olympics is to ensure that a full continuum of sport opportunities is available to people with mental handicaps. The following principles support this statement:
- Special Olympics provides sport opportunities directly for athletes with a mental handicap and links them with other organizations providing integrated sport opportunities.

- Special Olympics is a sport program. It involves both physical training and the matching of strength, endurance and physical skills in formalized settings with structured rules.

- The practice of grouping athletes for competition based on their abilities is fundamental and critical to the Special Olympics program. This practice ensures that all athletes experience equal competition.

- Training and preparation are essential to meaningful participation in sport and are indispensable elements of any Special Olympics program.

- Special Olympics uses sport to assist people with a mental handicap to become all that they can be — physically, mentally, socially, emotionally — and to become accepted, respected and productive members of society.

- Special Olympics may contain elements of play, recreation or physical education and should assist athletes in participating meaningfully and successfully in all dimensions of a physically active lifestyle.

- Special Olympics rewards dedication, preparation, effort and spirit ("doing your best" both in training and competition). Success is measured by the effect of the experience on the athlete.

CANADIAN WHEELCHAIR SPORTS ASSOCIATION
CWSA

A Brief History

Wheelchair sport was first introduced to the world in 1944 as a form of treatment and rehabilitation for the spinal-cord injured. It was conceived by Sir Ludwig Guttmann at the Stoke Mandeville Hospital in Aylesbury, England. Within four years the idea of sport as therapy developed into sport for competition and the striving for excellence. The annual World Stoke Mandeville Wheelchair Games were born.

In Canada, the development of wheelchair sport began as early as 1947. In 1967 the Canadian Wheelchair Sports Association (CWSA) was officially formed in Winnipeg, Manitoba, as a result of organizing for the first Pan Am Wheelchair Games. CWSA governs athletics, rugby and tennis and supports the development of archery, basketball, racquetball, shooting and swimming. The CWSA technical programs develop athletes and teams that represent the country nationally and internationally against the best in the world. The Canadian team consistently ranks among the top five internationally.

CWSA in the 1990s

Nationally, CWSA had 10 provincial associations that were responsible for conducting competitive and recreational programs to meet the needs of wheelchair athletes in each region. In all, over 3000 members were involved in activities and programs. Internationally, CWSA was a leader in the development of wheelchair sport. Canada is one of over 70 countries that are members of the International Stoke Mandeville

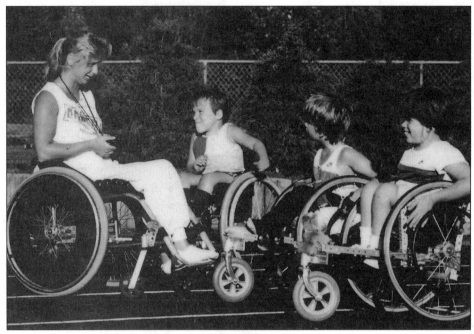

Young athletes at the CWSA Junior Sportsfest with Andrea Vadgson (left).

Wheelchair Sports Federation (ISMWSF), the world governing body for wheelchair sports.

CWSA operated for many years as a volunteer, not-for-profit organization on an annual budget of over $750,000. Approximately 30 percent of this amount came from athlete Rick Hansen's Man in Motion Legacy Fund (Hansen wheeled around the world to raise funds for research and awareness of people with spinal cord injuries); another 30 percent was funded by Sport Canada. The remaining 40 percent came from a combination of corporate sponsorship, donations and fund-raising. In the late 1990s, the stature and funding of CWSA was dramatically diminished, and CWSA offices closed in the spring of 1997.

Following is an interview conducted by journalist Chris Bourne with Colin Timm, former director of CWSA (Timm now works with Athletics Canada).

What was the role of your organization?

CWSA's mission was "Promoting Excellence and Developing Opportunities in Wheelchair Sport." CWSA was a membership-driven organization. We were in business to provide services to our members and affiliates. CWSA was one member of an extensive network of partners who promoted excellence and develop opportunities in wheelchair sports.

How did your organization influence, support and facilitate sporting opportunities for persons with a disability in Canada?

Wheelchair sport began to be developed in 1947, and the Canadian Wheelchair Sports Association was officially formed in 1967 in Winnipeg, Manitoba. CWSA governed athletics, rugby and tennis. From 1991 on, CWSA actively pursued the inclusion of wheelchair sports with the equivalent able-bodied sports. As a result, archery, racquetball, shooting and swimming have become fully integrated, at the national level, with their able-bodied counterparts. As well, in 1993 wheelchair basketball athletes formed their own national governing body — the Canadian Wheelchair Basketball Association (CWBA).

CWSA had provincial associations as well as a national one. Nationally, it provided technical, programming and administrative support to national- and international-level athletes.

What were the challenges facing your organization?

In the late 1990s, the CWSA faced a tremendous challenge in the area of funding. Two of our primary funding partners, Man In Motion (MIM) and Sport Canada, changed their funding priorities. MIM grants to wheelchair sports were no longer available; instead, the MIM Foundation was providing "services in kind." This meant a loss of up to one-third of CWSA's annual revenue.

Sport Canada funds were becoming increasingly less available as well. Sport Canada had indicated that its priority was to "fast-track" the integration of sports for athletes with a disability with the equivalent sports for able-bodied athletes. This means that Sport Canada no longer funded more than one organization that offered programs in the same sport (for example: Wheelchair Athletics was merged with Athletics Canada, and Wheelchair Tennis with Tennis Canada).

These changes had a drastic impact on the type and amount of funding available to support wheelchair sport programs and services in Canada. In order to ensure that our members continued to have access to services, CWSA pursued the concept of a secretariat for athletes with a disability. This secretariat will combine some or all national disability sport organizations into one organization that delivers services to Canada's athletes with a disability.

ORGANIZER PROFILE

Vic Cue

Birthdate: 1929

Birthplace: Calgary, AB

Current Residence: Vancouver, BC

Years of Involvement: 1962-1979

PHOTO: *Vic Cue in 1965 as coach of the Dueck Powerglides.*

■ CAREER HIGHLIGHT

Fundraising and organizing to enable Canada to send a team to the 1968 Paralympics in Tel Aviv, Israel

Vic Cue was born in Calgary in 1929, moved to West Vancouver three months later and has lived there ever since. He attended high school in West Vancouver and received a degree in physical education from the University of British Columbia in 1951.

Vic became involved in wheelchair sports when his brother introduced Vic to Doug Mowatt. Mowatt was looking for a wheelchair basketball coach for the Dueck Powerglides in Vancouver. Vic agreed to take on the task. "I had played a lot of basketball and it was my favourite sport," remembers Vic.

Many famous athletes came out of the BC wheel-chair basketball program, including Terry Fox, Rick Hansen, Eugene Reimer and Peter Collistro.

The Dueck Powerglides had formed in 1950 and were the first wheelchair basketball team in Canada. In the beginning they played exclusively in the United States against teams from Seattle, Tacoma and California. It was not until 1967, at the Montreal World Expo, that the Powerglides had the opportunity to play another Canadian team, the Montreal Wheelchair Wonders. Vic successfully coached the Dueck Powerglides and the Vancouver Cablecars from 1961 until 1978. During these years the Powerglides won nine Canadian championships. Many famous athletes came out of the BC wheelchair basketball program, including Terry Fox, Rick Hansen, Eugene Reimer and Peter Collistro.

It was also in 1967 that Canada was asked to host the first ever Pan American Wheelchair Games. Because of a shortage of funds and a mail strike, much of the organization and communication for this event took place via shortwave radio across Canada. "Prior to the Pan Ams in 1967, we had track meets across the country and all of the results were sent in to Winnipeg by ham radio operators. That was the way the team was picked," remembers Vic. "It was a big undertaking, considering we had no experience in that field."

To coincide with the hosting of the 1967 Pan American Wheelchair Games, the Canadian Wheelchair Sports Association was formed. Al Simpson in Winnipeg and Doug Mowatt in Vancouver were the prime movers in the formation of CWSA. Vic was invited to be the first athletic director for CWSA, a position he held until 1977.

One of the highlights of Vic's tenure with the CWSA was the 1968 Paralympic Games in Tel Aviv, Israel. Fund-raising for this event had been based in Ontario, but finding money wasn't easy — obtaining funds was an ongoing problem for wheelchair sports in the early days. "Three days before the team was supposed to leave for Tel Aviv," recalls Vic, "the group in the east phoned us to say they hadn't raised any money. Doug Mowatt went to the bank and signed a promissory note for $35,000 to take the team to the games. It would never have happened if Doug Mowatt hadn't done this." Through perseverance and personal connections — such as Doug Mowatt's relationship with Denny Boyd, the *Vancouver Sun* columnist — BC Wheelchair Sports was able to raise the funds to pay off the bank loan. Recalls Vic, "On returning from Israel, the BC Wheelchair Sports Association took over the loan and paid it off. If this had not happened, wheelchair sports would have been set back a number of years."

ORGANIZER PROFILE

gary
mcpherson

Birthplace: Edmonton, AB

Current Residence: Edmonton, AB

Years of Involvement: 1967 to present

PHOTO: Gary McPherson at the 1972 Paralympics in Germany.

■ CAREER HIGHLIGHTS

From 1974-78, served as executive director of the CWSA; elected president in 1985 and served until 1993

Gary McPherson became involved in wheelchair sports in 1967 through his skill as an amateur radio operator. The involvement came about as the result of a mail strike during the preparations for the first Pan American Wheelchair Games, which were scheduled to be held at the University of Alberta in the summer of 1967. In the absence of mail delivery, amateur (or "ham") radio was used extensively for cross-Canada communication, allowing the organizers to co-ordinate entries, classifications, accommodations, travel and myriad other details.

Gary became officially involved in wheelchair sport administration in 1972, when he was drafted to run for the presidency of the local Paralympic Sports Association. In 1974 he became the executive director of the CWSA. He served in that capacity until December 1978, then was treasurer until he left the organization in 1982. At the time Gary thought his career in wheelchair sports was over, but in 1985 he was approached to run for the presidency of CWSA. He served as president until November 1993 and represented CWSA at several international meetings, including one at Stoke Mandeville and the founding meeting of the International Paralympic Committee (IPC) in Dusseldorf, Germany, in 1989.

Before and during his term as President of CWSA, Gary was extensively involved in wheelchair basketball and other disability sports, both provincially and nationally. He was the co-ordinator of the second Canadian Games for the Physically Disabled, held in Edmonton in 1977 at the University of Alberta, and he was the general manager of the Alberta Northern Lights Wheelchair Basketball Society from December 1978 until April 1987. During that time the Northern Lights evolved from a club team to one of the best teams in North America. Gary also managed Canadian teams that competed at the 1979 and 1983 World Championships (known as the Gold Cup) in wheelchair basketball.

Among the events he attended over the years are the following competitions:
- 1972 Wheelchair Games in Calgary
- 1972 Paralympics in Heidelberg, Germany
- 1973 Wheelchair Games in Vancouver
- 1975 Wheelchair Games in Montreal
- 1976 First Canadian Games for the Physically Disabled in Cambridge, ON
- 1976 First International Paralympic Games in Etobicoke, ON involving all three disability groups
- 1977 Canadian Games in Edmonton
- 1978 Canadian Games in St. John's, NF
- 1979 Gold Cup in Tampa, Florida
- 1983 Gold Cup in Halifax, NS
- 1982 Pan American Wheelchair Games in Halifax

Gary was a member of the organizing committee for the 1994 Gold Cup, which was held in Edmonton. He has also served as a board member for the Canadian Federation of Sports Organizations for the Disabled (CFSOD) and the Canadian Paralympic Committee (CPC). His personal accomplishments in recent years include serving as chair of the Premier's Council on the Status of Persons with Disabilities for the province of Alberta from 1988 until June 1998. He was also assistant director of the Fitness and Lifestyle Center for the physically disabled, now known as the Rick Hansen Centre, at the University of Alberta. Currently Gary is an employee of the University of Alberta and director of the newly created Centre for Voluntary Enterprise and Social Entrepreneurship in the Faculty of Business. He is also an adjunct professor, special lecturer and advisor in the Faculty of Physical Education and Recreation at the university.

His greatest disappointment with the CWSA is that the organization has failed to attract and nurture new volunteers.

When asked about his greatest personal disappointment, Gary cites the fact that the CWSA appears to be a shadow of itself when compared to its strength in the late 1980s and early 1990s. He takes responsibility for not ensuring that there was an adequate succession process in place to sustain the CWSA. Unfortunately, organizational politics, personalities and provincial biases made it difficult. He acknowledges that this kind of systemic difficulty takes a lot of time and insight to resolve. If he were involved with CWSA today, he says, he would be better prepared, personally, to tackle this challenge. However, he has moved on to another chapter in his life and has different immediate priorities.

His greatest disappointment with the CWSA is that the organization has failed to attract and nurture new volunteers. This has resulted in a deterioration of administrative capability within wheelchair sport specifically, and sport for athletes with a disability generally. The performance of athletes has far surpassed the capabilities of the voluntary administration.

In looking to the future, Gary affirms that he will always be a friend of the sporting movement for athletes with disabilities. Today he devotes a great deal of his time to his family, trying to instill in his children the value of teamwork and leadership and sharing the many lessons he's learned through his involvement in sport.

frick

Birthplace: Sudbury, ON

Current Residence: Port Coquitlam, BC

Coach: Wheelchair Basketball

■ CAREER HIGHLIGHT

Participated in building the national women's wheelchair basketball program

Tim Frick, who is now in his forties, has been involved in coaching wheelchair sports for over 20 years. He lives in Port Coquitlam, British Columbia, but grew up in Sudbury and Parksville, Ontario. He is currently an instructor in Coaching and Sport Science at Douglas College, and lives with wife Gerry Phillips and a large (Malinois-Shepherd cross) dog.

Following is a recent interview conducted by the author with Tim Frick.

How, when and where did you first get involved in disability sport?
I first got involved through the University of British Columbia (UBC) in 1975 or 1976. I volunteered at a basketball game between the Cablecars and a US team (I think it was Sacramento). Then I met Rick Hansen in 1976 through a mutual volleyball-playing friend, Glen Burrell. In 1977 I helped with the BC Games held at UBC in the summer of that year.

"I struck up a friendship with Rick Hansen and was coerced into coaching wheelchair volleyball."

Was there any one particular person who inspired you to get involved?
Well, I struck up a friendship with Rick Hansen and was coerced into coaching wheelchair volleyball. I agreed to try it for two weeks but only upon the condition that I would not adjust my coaching style just because the athletes were in wheelchairs. I told the team that after two weeks, if they didn't like it then I'd leave with no hard feelings. And here I am, 21 years later...

Can you tell us some of the sports and activities you have been involved in other than wheelchair basketball and volleyball?
I was involved in volleyball from 1977 to 1981. At the same time I coached Rick and others — Ron Minor, Mel Fitzgerald, Andre Viger and Diane Rackiecki, to name a few

— in wheelchair track and marathoning. This was from 1977 to 1984. I also provided some advisory assistance to Terry Fox when he was training for his cross-country run, and I've given "quadrugby" clinics. And I coached powerlifter Lenny Marriott to a Canadian record in weightlifting.

What do you see as your greatest accomplishment in sport?

My greatest accomplishment was building the national women's wheelchair basketball team into a well-functioning and highly skilled group of basketball players.

What do you see as your greatest disappointment?

Not having the resources to spend more time coaching.

What is the most significant barrier facing athletes with disabilities at your level of competition?

Ther biggest problem right now is that there are not quite enough high-level competitive events.

Do you have any thoughts about the direction of disability sport in the future?

I think we need to continue to grow and develop, and to collaborate with others to meet everyone's needs. On the positive side, the Rick Hansens, Stan Stronges and Reg McClellans of the sport have made it easy for people like me to achieve personal goals. I would like to thank them for believing in me and for giving so much of themselves so that others could benefit.

3

Appendices

CHRONOLOGY OF EVENTS IN THE DEVELOPMENT OF DISABILITY SPORT

1939: • George Stafford publishes "Sport for the Handicapped" at the University of Illinois.

1945: • War Veterans return home from World War II.

1947: • First "informal" competition in Canada takes place at Deer Lodge Hospital, Manitoba. Events include: archery, milk bottle pitching, basketball throw, ring toss, croquet and golf putting.

1948: • First Stoke Mandeville Games are held, involving 16 competitors in Aylesbury, England.

1949: • National Wheelchair Basketball Association is formed in the United States.

1952: • Wheelchair basketball program is started in Vancouver by Stan Stronge. The Dueck Powerglides play American teams; no other Canadian teams exist yet.
• Second Stoke Mandeville Games take place, involving 130 athletes, including athletes from Great Britain and the Netherlands.

1953: • Bill Hepburn forms the Montreal Wheelchair Wonders. The Montreal team represents Canada in the Third Stoke Mandeville Games, marking Canada's start in world competition.

1954: • Montreal Wheelchair Wonders represent Canada at the sixth National Wheelchair Basketball Tournament in New York, N.Y.

1956: • The Fearnley Cup, an Olympic award for outstanding achievement, is presented at the Stoke Mandeville Games.

1960: • First Summer Paralympic Event takes place in Rome, Italy, using Olympic venues.

1962: • Jerry Johnston begins to teach skiers with disabilities in Banff, Alberta.
• First Commonwealth Games for athletes with a disability take place in Perth, Australia.
• Toronto researcher and professor Dr. Frank Hayden works with children with mental handicaps to increase their fitness levels.

1963: • First interprovincial wheelchair basketball event takes place in Saskatoon, Saskatchewan.
• International Sport Organisation for the Disabled (ISOD) is formed.
• Eunice Kennedy Shriver starts a summer day-camp for children and adults with mental disabilities at her home in Maryland, exploring their capabilities in a variety of sports and physical activities.

1964: • Dr Robert Jackson witnesses the Tokyo Paralympic event and vows to send a Canadian team to the next Paralympics.

1966: • Second Commonwealth Games take place in Kingston, Jamaica. Canada sends one athlete — Ben Reimer of Winnipeg, Manitoba. Reimer wins a bronze medal in the javelin.
      • Ludwig Guttman, founder of the Stoke Mandeville Games, receives knighthood from Queen Elizabeth II.

Pan American Wheelchair Games in Winnipeg, 1967.

1967: • Pan American Wheelchair Games take place in Winnipeg, Manitoba.
      • Canada's wheelchair athletes compete against each other at the Montreal Centennial Games. Canadian Wheelchair Sports Association is formed during this event, and Dr. Robert Jackson is elected as chair.

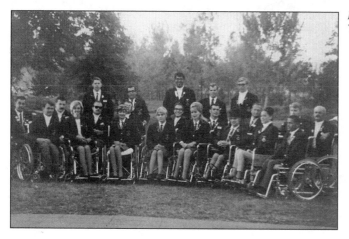

First Canadian Paralympic Team, Tel Aviv, 1968.

1968: • Canada sends its first Paralympic team to Tel Aviv, Israel with 22 wheelchair athletes. First National Wheelchair Games take place in Edmonton, Alberta.
      • Irene Miller is named Manitoba's Sportswoman of the Year.
      • International Special Olympics is founded by Eunice Kennedy Shriver in the USA. Canada is represented by a Floor Hockey Team from Toronto at the first International Special Olympics Games held at Soldier Field in Chicago.

Canadian Pan American Team in Argentina, 1969.

1969: • Second National Wheelchair Games takes place in Hamilton, Ontario.
• Canada sends 17 athletes to the Second Pan American Wheelchair Games in Buenos Aries, Argentina.
• The first Canadian Special Olympics (CSO) Games and National Hockey League (NHL) Floor Hockey Tournament are held in Toronto

1970: • Western Canada Wheelchair Games take place in Penticton, BC. National Wheelchair Games are not held due to financial constraints.

1971: • Third National Wheelchair Games take place in Montreal, Quebec,

BC Athletes leaving for the 1972 Paralympics in Germany.

1972: • Canada sends a wheelchair team to the Heidelberg Paralympics.
• Fourth National Wheelchair Games take place in Calgary, Alberta.
• Seven Canadian provinces hold local, regional and provincial Special Olympics events.

1973: • Eugene Reimer, an athlete with a disability, is awarded the title of Canadian Male Athlete of the Year.
• Fifth Wheelchair Games take place in Vancouver, BC.
• Fourth Pan American Games take place in Lima, Peru. Richard Wasnock of British Columbia wins the Best Male Athlete award.

1974: • Sixth Wheelchair Games take place in Winnipeg, Manitoba.
   • Canadian Special Olympics are incorporated as a national, charitable volunteer organization.

1975: • Doug Lyons of Drummondville, Quebec is named Quebec Athlete of the Year.
   • Diane Crowe Earl becomes the first person with a disability to complete a bachelor's degree in Physical Education.
   • Seventh National Wheelchair Games take place in Montreal, Quebec.
   • Canada is represented by 138 Special Olympians at the Fourth International Special Olympics Games held in Mount Pleasant, Michigan.

1976: • The Toronto Olympiad for the Physically Disabled takes place. Canada hosts its first Paralympic Games but federal funding is withdrawn due to the presence of South African athletes. Polish team withdraw partway through the games and several athletes defect.
   • Arnie Boldt is named Outstanding Athlete of the Toronto Olympiad; Boldt is runner-up to Greg Joy as Canada's Outstanding Senior Male Athlete of 1976.
   • Canadian Amputee Sports Association, Canadian Blind Sports Association and Canadian Association of Disabled Skiers are formed.
   • First Canadian Games for the Physically Disabled are held in Cambridge, Ontario.
   • First Winter Paralympics are held in Oshevik, Sweden.
   • First wheelchair tennis tournament is held in Los Angeles, California, USA.

1977: • Second Canadian Games for the Physically Disabled are held in Edmonton, Alberta.

BC's Rick Hansen competing at the Canadian Games for the Physically Disabled in 1978.

1978: • Canadian Games for the Physically Disabled are held in St. John's, Newfoundland. The games become a bi-annual event.
   • Saskatchewan Special Olympics Society host the invitational National Special Olympics Games in Regina. Five hundred athletes — some from every province in Canada — participate.

Doug Lyons from Quebec competing in the Canadian Games for the Physically Disabled in 1978.

1979: • Wheelchair Basketball hosts its own national championship separate from the multisport games.
      • Canadian Special Olympics chapters are incorporated in New Brunswick, Nova Scotia and Ontario. Two hundred and seventy athletes take part in the Nova Scotia Special Olympics Summer Games held in New Glasgow. The first Ontario Special Olympics Summer Games are held in Etobicoke and 440 athletes participate.

1980: • Canadian National Championships for Blind and Amputee Athletes are held.
      • Terry Fox, an amputee, starts his Marathon of Hope run across Canada, to raise funds for cancer research.
      • Summer Paralympics are held in Arnhem, Holland. Second Winter Paralympics are held in Geilo, Norway and Lana Spreeman wins the first gold medal for Canada.
      • Canadian Special Olympics chapters are incorporated in Manitoba, Alberta and British Columbia. New Brunswick Special Olympics organise Summer Games in Moncton for 500 athletes.

1981: • Canada Games for the Physically Disabled are held in Scarborough, Ontario. Wheelchair, blind and amputee athletes compete.
      • International Blind Sports Association (IBSA) is formed.
      • Rick Hansen wins the wheelchair division of the Vancouver International Marathon.

1982: • Pan American Wheelchair Games are held in Halifax, Nova Scotia; amputee athletes are allowed to compete. Gary Collins Simpson of Vancouver brings back several gold medals in swimming.
      • Separate National Championships, to be held once a year, are established for each disability group.

1983: • Canadian Games for the Physically Disabled take place in Sudbury, Ontario.
      • Diane Rakiecki becomes the first female Canadian wheelchair athlete to complete a marathon.

Rick Hansen in 1982, with the BC Wheelchair Athlete of the Year Award.

- Canada is represented by the second largest team at the International Special Olympics Summer Games at Louisiana State University in Baton Rouge. Canada sends 135 athletes and 44 coaches to compete among the 4,500 athletes from 51 participating countries.

1984: • The magazine *Palaestra: The Forum of Sport and Physical Education for the Disabled* features Arnold Boldt on the cover of its first issue.
- International Games for the Physically Disabled are held in New York, NY.
- Wheelchair athletes from Canada compete in Stoke Mandeville Games.
- Phil Chew represents Canada at the demonstration skiing event at the Sarejevo Winter Olympics.
- Los Angeles Summer Olympics feature demonstration events for wheelchair track; Mel Fitzgerald, Rick Hansen and Andre Viger represent Canada in the men's 1500m; Debbie Kostelyk and Diane Rackeicki represent Canada in the women's 800m.
- Wheelchair athlete Rick Hansen starts his Man in Motion World Tour, which will take him around the world and radically increase public awareness of athletes with a disability.
- Third Winter Paralympics take place in Innsbruck, Austria.
- Special Olympics Inc. awards Canadian Special Olympics Honourary Head Coach Lanny McDonald the International Special Olympics Award for Distinguished Service to mentally handicapped people.

1985: • Canadian Games for the Physically Disabled are held in Sault Ste Marie, Ontario. First demonstration of wheelchair tennis takes place at these games.
- World Cup of Goalball is held in Calgary, Alberta.
- First Sledge Hockey Nationals are held in Ottawa, Ontario.

1986: • World Championships for the Physically Disabled take place in Goteborg, Sweden. Canada sends a strong contingent of blind, amputee and wheelchair athletes.
- Canadian Special Olympics Summer Games are held in Calgary, Alberta. Eight hundred athletes and 200 coaches participate.
- A Canadian Special Olympics Chapter is incorporated in Newfoundland and Labrador.
- Ian Gregson becomes the first Canadian athlete with a disability to earn a post-secondary athletic scholarship (at Simon Fraser University in Vancouver, BC).

1987: • Canadian Games for the Physically Disabled take place in Brantford, Ontario. Wheelchair tennis is included as a medal sport at these games.
• Canadian athletes compete at the International Games in Paris, France.
• Wheelchair athlete Andre Viger wins his third Boston Marathon.
• Rick Hansen returns home after wheeling 24,901.55 miles through 34 countries. Simon Fraser University establishes the Rick Hansen Award, the first Canadian post-secondary athletic scholarship for athletes with a disability.

1988: • At the Seoul Paralympics,Canada wins 159 medals, finishing fourth overall.
• Separate National Championships for Wheelchair Tennis are held in Ottawa, Ontario.
• Fourth Winter Paralympics are held in Innsbruck, Austria.

1989: • Canadian Foresters Games take place in Richmond, BC. Wheelchair Tennis Nationals are held during these games.
• International Special Olympics Winter Games were held in Reno and Lake Tahoe; 70 athletes and coaches make up the Canadian Team, who bring home 20 gold, 13 silver and 11 bronze medals.

1990: • World Championships for the Physically Disabled are held in Assen, Holland.
• Wheelchair Tennis Nationals take place in Saskatoon, Saskatchewan.
• Canadian Special Olympics Summer Games are hosted by Vancouver, BC. One thousand athletes and coaches, representing all the provinces and the Yukon, attend.

1991: • Canadian Foresters Games are held in Brantford, Ontario.
• Wheelchair Tennis Nationals are held in Fredericton, New Brunswick.
• First World Cup of Sledge Hockey takes place in Oslo, Norway; Team Canada wins gold.

1992: • Barcelona Paralympics are held and Canadians bring back 75 medals and finish 6th overall. Canada women win wheelchair-basketball gold. Joanne Mucz of Manitoba wins five gold medals in swimming and sets five new world records.
• The 1500m wheelchair race becomes an Olympic demonstration sport. Canadian Jeff Adams competes in the race.
• Second World Cup of Sledge Hockey takes place. Canada hosts the World Cup as part of the Canadian Winter Games for the Physically Disabled in Ottawa. Team Canada wins gold.
• First Canadian National Track and Field Championship for the Disabled takes place in Abbotsford, BC. Blind, amputee and cerebral palsy athletes compete.
• Wheelchair Tennis Nationals are held in Winnipeg, Manitoba.
• Fifth Winter Paralympics are held in Tignes, France.

1993: • Vista 93 Conference takes place in Edmonton, Alberta.

1994: • Canada hosts the Commonwealth Games in Victoria, BC. Athletes with various disabilities compete in four sports. Jeff Adams wins the 1500m wheelchair race, while Andrew Haley wins the 100m freestyle swim. HRH Prince Andrew presents Haley with his medal. Australian Chef de Mission Arthur Tunstall retracts his statement about disabled athletes being "an embarrassment."

- World Championships in various sports are held in various locations: track and field, Berlin; Powerlifting, Upsalla, Sweden. Several events are postponed due to financial limitations.
- Sixth Winter Paralympics take place in Lillehammer, Norway. Sledge hockey is included for the first time; Canada wins bronze.

- 1995: Canadian Track and Field Championship for the Physically Disabled is held in Saint John, New Brunswick. Blind, amputee and cerebral palsy athletes compete.
- Jeff Adams wins the demonstration 1500m wheelchair event at the International Amateur Athletic Federation World Championships in Goteborg Sweden.
- Malaysian Commonwealth Games Organising Committee decides not to include athletes with a disability in the 1998 Commonwealth Games. Manchester Commonwealth Games Organising Committee announce they will host athletes with a disability at the 2002 Commonwealth Games.
- 25th Anniversary of Canadian Special Olympics is celebrated.
- Special Olympics Bowling Championships are held in Calgary, Alberta.

- 1996: Atlanta Paralympics are held; Canada brings back 69 medals.
- World Championship of Sledge Hockey takes place in Nynasham, Sweden. Canada wins bronze.
- Colette Bourgonje receives Canadian Association for the Advancement of Women Sport (CAAWS) Individual Breakthrough Award for having "pushed the limits" for athletes with a disability.

1997: • men's 1500m and women's 800m track events are rejected for full medal status at the 2000 Olympics. Canadian Dick Pound supports the decision.
- Rick Hansen celebrates a decade of Man in Motion with a mini cross-country tour which culminates at GM Place in Vancouver.
- Dick pound becomes a member of the International Olympic Committee.
- Special Olympics World Winter Games take place in Toronto and Collingwood, Ontario.

1998: • Canadian Special Olympics Summer Games are held in Sudbury, Ontario.

1998: • Winter Paralympics are held in Nagano, Japan. Canada's Patrick Jarvis becomes first former Paralympic athlete to become Chef de Mission of a Paralympic team. Canadian athletes bring home numerous medals.
- In September, the Commonwealth Games are held in Kuala Lumpur. Athletes with a disability are not invited to attend.

2000: • Paralympics held in Sydney, Australia.

2002: • Manchester, Commonwealth Games held in Manchester, England. Athletes with disabilites are scheduled to attend even more events than they did in Victoria, Canada in 1994.

THE BANNING OF ATHLETES WITH A DISABILITY

When one thinks of "bans" in Canadian sport one usually thinks of Ben Johnson or other Olympic calibre athletes being banned from competition for taking illegal substances. The sad truth is that you do not have to have take illegal substances to be banned from competing in a sport in Canada; you merely have to have a disability. There are numerous instances of "legitimate" rules preventing people with disabilities from taking part in sporting and recreational events. While the rules that govern sport have not been written with a potential athlete's disability in mind, they are often used as a tool to prevent participation by athletes with a disability.

One example of this use of the rules can be found in track and field, where a crouch start is required in the 100, 200 and 400m races. According to the rules, all four limbs must be in contact with the ground for a legal start. If an athlete is missing a right arm, it is impossible for him or her to have all four limbs in contact with the ground. Enforcing these rules to the letter means that an athlete with an amputation of the arm is not allowed to compete — and the reality is that such rules are enforced verbatim, not only in Canada but all over the world. Similarly, a rule enforced at swimming events requires a swimmer to turn with both feet at the end of the lap. What happens to the swimmer who has no feet or no use of the feet? In baseball, one rule states that no foreign objects are allowed on the field of play. In the early 1980s, the rule was enforced to the point where a coach who used a wheelchair was banned from the field of play because his chair was a "foreign object." This argument was taken to court and the coach in the wheelchair won the right to enter the field.

Another source of debate is the use of prostheses. In the 1970s, a talented above-knee amputee competed at non-disability shooting meets. At first no one had much of an argument against his participation. With the increased level of competition the amputee shooter got better and better, to the point where he became eligible to compete for Canada at the 1976 Olympics in Montreal. Their egos bruised, officials and competitors alike complained that the amputee's prosthesis gave him an unfair advantage over his fellow shooters. The officials determined that the prosthesis was a "support" device and, since support devices where not allowed at shooting events, he was banned from competing and missed an opportunity to attend the Olympics.

Most recently, the International Powerlifting Federation (IPF) has decreed that prostheses and leg braces are pieces of equipment, not part of the human anatomy. Apparently, the fact that most prosthesis users consider their artificial limb to be part of their anatomy is irrelevant. It was arbitrarily decided that the prosthesis belongs on the list of unacceptable equipment (such as shoes, belts and wraps). Even leg-brace users were out of luck: the amputee could remove the leg prosthesis but this action meant that the competitor contravened yet another rule stating that a lifter must keep "both" feet flat on the floor.

While this interpretation of rules may have legitimacy in the eyes of those who enforce them, the reality is that the rules are a barrier to fair participation by athletes with a disability in certain sport events. One particularly horrifying story involved Ken Doyle (see profile) a young powerlifter from Nova Scotia who travelled all the way to Finland to compete at the International Powerlifting Federation Bench Press World Championship. Apparently no one told the lifter that leg braces were regarded as illegal equipment until it was time for that lifter to compete. The lifter was informed after his first attempt that he would have to remove his leg braces in order to make a second and third attempt. Without any means of accessing the lifting platform, the lifter was forced to crawl to the platform and, because of the time constraints on competitors, missed his second and third attempts. The lifter has since given up all hope of ever competing in non-disability bench press events. Ironically, this lifter still holds the Canadian junior record in his weight class for the bench press.

This lack of regard for basic human rights and equal, fair athletic competition is often described as "the level playing field." How far do you have to go to make the playing field level for everyone? Some Canadian sports organisations are willing to go further than others to help athletes with a disability compete on an equal basis, where possible. Many, however, are steadfast in their belief that any change in the rules will open the doors to a flood of change that will irrevocably destroy their sport. There is a paradox at the heart of this refusal to change: often, a disability is interpreted as a handicap only if the result at the end of the day favours the non-disabled. As soon as the result is reversed (i.e. the athlete with a disability wins) the disability somehow becomes an advantage.

Canadian disability sport organisations are ill-equipped to deal with bans and unfair treatment. Too often, they give only "moral support" to athletes struggling with these situations. Too often, they are willing to let the passage of time fix the problem. Time maybe a great healer of emotional wounds, but if problems can be resolved only when athletes finally lose heart, this hardly resolves the dispute in a fair and equitable manner.

Canadian non-disability sport organisations must realise that encouraging athletes with a disability to compete against their non-disabled counterparts can only benefit the sport. The athlete with a disability has to overcome physical limitations in order to compete on an equal basis with non-disabled athletes, and the ability to overcome such limitations should not be used against that athlete.

In some sports, some athletes with a disability have the inherent ability to compete on an equal basis with their non-disabled counterparts. As a society, we must strive to remove the barriers that prevent equal participation in these sports. Athletes and officials must recognise that athletes with a disability can compete equitably with other athletes — and may even win.

THE CLASSIFICATION DEBATE

I deally, the classification system for athletes with a disability allows athletes with similar functional or sensory levels to compete on an equal basis. Unfortunately, the classification system has yet to remain constant from one Paralympic event to the next. The system is constantly evolving, sometimes to the detriment of some athletes and the benefit of others.

Early classification systems developed by the International Stoke Mandeville Wheelchair Sports Federation (ISMWSF) are no longer used within the International Paralympic Committee (IPC) sports system. Until 1992, classification systems were based on specific disabilities. Since 1992, the classification system has become more (although not completely) sport based. There has also been an effort to reduce the number of classes.

This effort has benefitted some athletes while making fair competition virtually impossible for others.

The effort to reduce classifications has worked in sports such as swimming and powerlifting, where the level of competition has increased dramatically. In sports such as track and field, however, competitors in events for women have continually found themselves competing within merged classes and this has resulted in unfair advantages for the higher functioning athletes.

In general, it is acceptable for amputees to compete against paraplegics and athletes with cerebral palsy (CP) in some sports such as swimming and powerlifting, but not in others such as track and field. The classification system for the blind and visually impaired has undergone little change since its inception in the mid-1970s. Officially, blind and visually impaired athletes do not compete against amputees, paraplegics or athletes with CP. Unofficially, however, it is not unheard of for all classifications to compete in the same event at regional and local levels in order to foster some level of competition.

Classification remains a hotly debated issue within the disability sport community and is guaranteed to change, often depending on who "shouts" the loudest. For this reason, classification remains the part of disability sport that is least understood by the general public and sports writers.

What follows is an outline of the categories of classification, with a few examples of classification systems unique to individual sports.

CLASSIFICATION BY DISABILITY

Athletes who are Amputees
(1988 to the present day)
A1: Amputation of both legs above or through the knee joint
A2: Amputation of one leg above or through the knee joint
A3: Amputation of both legs below the knee
A4: Amputation of one leg below the knee joint
A5: Amputation of both arms above or through the elbow
A6: Amputation of one arm above or through the elbow
A7: Amputation of both arms below the elbow but through or above the wrist joint
A8: Amputation of one arm below the elbow but through or above the wrist joint; combined lower and upper limb amputations
A9: Congenital amputations of hands or feet, functionally classified by the medical technical committee

Athletes who are Blind
(1988 to the present day)
Standard definition of blindness: less than 10 percent useful vision.
B1: No light perception at all in either eye, or some light perception in one or both eyes accompanied by an inability to recognize objects or contours in any direction and at any distance.
B2: Ability to recognize objects or contours with a visual acuity of up to 2/60, or with a limitation of field of vision of five degrees.
B3: 2/60 and 6/60 vision, or field of vision between five and 20 degrees.

Athletes with Cerebral Palsy (CP)

(1988 to the present day)

Class 1 (C1):

1. Moderate to severe spasticity in all four limbs.
2. Poor functional strength in upper extremities and torso, necessitating the use of an electric wheelchair or personal assistance for regular daily use.
3. Cannot push a manual wheelchair with arms or legs.

Class 2 (C2):

1. Moderate to severe involvement in all four limbs.
2. Normally wheelchair bound. Cannot walk without assistance, or can walk only with extreme difficulty.
3. Have poor functional strength and severe control problems in the upper extremities and torso.
4. Because of the varying functional abilities within this class, separate track and field events have been developed for the upper extremities and the lower extremities.

Class 3 (C3):

1. Moderate handicap in all four limbs or three limbs.
2. Have fair functional strength and moderate control problems in the upper extremities and torso.
3. Must use wheelchair for regular daily activities, but may be able to ambulate with the assistance of devices.

Class 4 (C4):

1. Good functional strength and minimal control problems in the upper extremities and torso.
2. Lower limbs have moderate to severe spasticity.
3. May be able to walk short distances with use of devices, but needs wheelchair for regular daily activities.

Class 5 (C5):

1. Both lower limbs have moderate to severe spasticity, resulting in difficulty with walking.
2. Right or left extremities may have moderate to severe spasticity causing difficulty with walking.
3. Have good functional strength and minimal control problems in upper extremities, or, in the case of the moderate hemiplegic, one arm and leg have functional strength while the affected side may have exaggerated reflexes.
4. May walk with or without aids, but may need to use wheelchair in some daily activities.

Class 6 (C6):

1. Moderate to severe control problems in all four limbs.
2. May walk without assistive devices during daily activities.
3. The athletes in this class have more control problems than those in Class 5, while Class 6 competitors may have better functioning lower extremities.

Class 7 (C7):

1. Moderate spasticity in one half of the body, or moderate to minimal spasticity in all four limbs.
2. Walk without assistive devices, but spasticity in lower limbs may cause limp when walking.

3. Usually have good functional ability in non-affected side of hemiplegic.

Class 8 (C8):

1. May include a minimally affected hemiplegic, monoplegic or very minimally involved quadriplegic.
2. Able to run and jump freely.
3. May have minimal loss of full function caused by lack of coordination.

Athletes Described as "Les Autres" (LA)

(The LA category includes athletes with polio, muscular dystrophy and spina bifida, as well as athletes with motor disabilities resulting from injuries to the musculoskeletal or nervous system.)

LA1: Uses wheelchair; poor sitting balance; reduced muscle strength and mobility in all limbs; asymmetry; prone to extreme fatigue.

LA2: Almost always uses a wheelchair; fair sitting balance and arm function; some leg function; some asymmetry; prone to extreme fatigue.

LA3: Walks with crutches and/or braces; some balance problems; occasional asymmetry; wheelchair user with good sitting balance; impaired arm and leg function.

LA4: Walks without crutches or braces; may use walking stick; some balance problems; reduced function in one leg and one arm, or in both arms and legs.

Sport-specific classification has been a trend since 1990. The basic premise behind sport-specific classification is to increase the level of competition in any given sport.

CLASSIFICATION BY SPORT

In track and field (commonly referred to as "athletics"), classification varies from one disability to the next and from one event to the next. The common factor is that T=track and F=field. Under this system, "T42" refers to an athlete who is an above-knee amputee who competes in track events; "F42" refers to an above-knee amputee who competes in field events. The number 42 represents the amputee class, which ranges from 40 to 49. The second digit in this number represents the level of amputation (1 to 9). Each disability has its own class of numbers.

Swimming has an even more complicated system in which swimmers are classified differently from one event to the next. For example, a swimmer can be classified as S9 in one event and SW8 in another. Theoretically, this creates equal competition by eliminating minor functional differences.

To complicate matters, variations on classification systems occur within Canada.

Examples of some sport classification systems are as follows:

Boccia

Boccia is played primarily by athletes with cerebral palsy (CP). The five medal events include: Individual Mixed Class I; Individual Mixed Class II; Team Mixed Classes C1 and C2 (see below); and Pairs Mixed Class.

Classifications:

Class 1 (C1): Quadriplegic dependent upon electric wheelchair or wheelchair assistance:

non-functional movement in lower extremities; non-existent or very poor trunk control; severe difficulty adjusting back to mid-line or upright position; severe limitation in upper extremity range of movement; reduced throwing motion with poor follow-through; opposition of thumb and one finger possible, allowing grip.
Class 2 (C2): Quadriplegic with poor strength in all extremities.

Wheelchair Athletics
International Stoke Mandeville Wheelchair Sports Federation Classifications (1980 to the present day)
   Abbreviations: • T = Thoracic   • L = Lumbar   • S = Sacral

Cervical Disabilities
   1A: Upper cervical lesions with triceps not functional against resistance.
   1B: Lower cervical lesions with good or normal power in the triceps, wrist extensors and flexors, but having no finger flexors or extensors of functional value.
   1C: Lower cervical lesions with good or normal triceps, strong finger flexors and extensors, but having no interossei or lumbrical musculature of functional value.

Thoracic Disabilities
   I: Having no useful balance when sitting (below T1 to T5 inclusive).
   II: Ability to maintain balance when sitting, ignoring lower abdominal muscles of non-functional strength (below T5 to T10 inclusive).
   III: Below T10 to L3 inclusive, provided that quadriceps power is non-functional.
   IV: Below L3 to S2 inclusive, provided that quadriceps power is Grade Three or above.
   V: (for swimmers only): 41-60 inclusive, traumatic; 36-50 inclusive, polio.

Wheelchair Basketball
Athletes with paraplegia, cerebral palsy (CP) and amputations, as well as those classified as les autres (LA) compete in wheelchair basketball.
Classification Rules:
   • Classification in wheelchair basketball measures the player's volume of action as opposed to his or her power, technique or ability.
   • There are four classifications for wheelchair basketball players. Most athletes fit into these classifications, although extenuating circumstances may warrant the issuance of a half-point classification.
   • The total combined point value of a team's players on the court may not exceed 14 at any time during play.
   Class A1: Unable to fix the pelvis; unable to perform active rotation of the trunk; lack abdominal muscles.
   Class A2: Unable to fix the pelvis; have trunk rotation and stability.
   Class A3: Able to fix the pelvis and move the trunk; good mobility in the frontal plane; able to lean forward and return to upright position without pushing the arms.
   Class A4: Able to fix the pelvis and move the trunk; active mobility in all planes; can lean to at least one side, using hips to maintain balance.

PARALYMPIC TEAMS SINCE 1980

1980: ARNHEM, HOLLAND

Gerald Regan — Minister Fitness and Amateur Sport

Chef de Mission — Robert D. Steadward
Asst Chef — Murray Minshall
Technical Consultant — Dick Loiselle
Amputee Team manager — Jim Fraser
Blind Team manager — Gerry York
Wheelchair Team manager H "Boots" Cooper

Medical Staff
Dr Norman Lush
Dr. Irv Grosfield
Dieter Bonas
Sharon McParland
Bill Wilcox

Equipment
Roy Brideau
Ron Urness
Tony van der Waarde
Merv Oveson

Office Staff
Ingrid Draayer
Sue Hamelin

Amputee Team
Asst. Team manager — Nancy Madeleine Anderson
Coach — Malcolm Bowman
Coach — Graham Knox
Coach — Bob Wade

Athletes
Sarah Baker — Field & Swimming
Stefania Balta — Field
Gisselle Cole — Athletics
Ann Farrell — Athletics
Karen Gillis — Athletics
Susie Grimstead — Field & Swimming
Cheryl Kristiansen — Swimming

Josee Lake — Swimming
Rose Ann McKinnon — Swimming
Jackie Mitchell — Swimming
Marg Nicholson — Swimming
Marj Seargeant — Swimming
Magella Belanger — Athletics
Arnie Boldt — Field
Gary Collins-Simpson — Swimming
George Crhak — Table Tennis
Les Decsi — Shooting
Chris Facey — Athletics
Larry Gardner — Swimming
Joe Harrison — Athletics
Al Heaver — Athletics
Gordon Huculiak — Athletics
Denis LaPalme — Athletics & Swimming
Sonny Lee — Table Tennis
Dan Leonard — Field
Phil Mindorff — Swimming
Peter Palubicki — Field
Charles Peart — Athletics
Tony Wills — Athletics
Dale Vincent — Field & Swimming

Blind Team

Coach — John Howe
Coach — Louis Michaud
Coach — Audrey Strom
Coach — Wilfred Strom
Coach — Linda Triff
Coach — Jim Leask
Guide Runner — Darell Menard
Guide Runner — Dominique Savard
Guide Runner — Robert Englehutt
Intervenor — Ian Kingsley
Intervenor — Don Gallow

Athletes

Lucille Baillargeon — Athletics
Lisa Bentz — Swimming
Susan Cox — Athletics
Cheryl Hurd — Athletics
Kim Kilpatrick — Athletics & Swimming
Danielle Lessard — Field
Yvette Michel — Swimming
Anna Ostapa — Athletics
Andrea Rossi — Swimming

Barbara Smith — Field
Tina Stevenson — Athletics
Lily Wong — Athletics
Bernard Bessette — Athletics & Swimming
Yvan Bourdeau — Athletics
Paul English — Track
Alan Farough — Swimming & Wrestling
Lee Grenon — Swimming
Rod Hersey — Athletics & Goalball
Terry Kelly — Track & Goallball
Eric Lambier — Track, Goalball & Wrestling
Craig MacFarlane — Track & Wrestling
Andre Mainville — Athletics
Gilles Marois — Athletics & Goallball
Tim McIsaac — Swimming
Eddie Morten — Athletics
Pier Morten — Wrestling
Carlos Pardo — Track
Jacques Pilon — Track
Peter Quaiattini — Swimming
Patrick York — Athletics & Swimming
Darrold Lindquist — Wrestling
John Knight — Wrestling
Vic Perreira — Wrestling
Charels Pond — Wrestling
Art Scott — Wrestling

Wheelchair Team

Head Coach — Donald Royer
Coach — Greg Eng
Coach — Tim Frick
Coach — Bill Lynes
Coach — Bill Mahony
Coach — Heather Snell
Coach — Patricia Wallace
Coach — Cathy Walsh
Coach — Graham Ward

Athletes

Darlene Edgett — Track
Elaine Ell — Field
Pamela Frazee — Swimming
Diane Leeming — Athletics
Joanne McDonald — Track & Table Tennis
Lucie Raiche — Field
Jacquelin Roy — Track
Sandy Sorenson — Track

Irene Wownuk — Swimming
Mark Burger — Track, Table Tennis & Swimming
Dennis Cherenko — Athletics
Paul Clark — Track
Peter Collistro — Basketball
John Donahue — Athletics
Fred Edney — Athletics
Mel Fitzgerald — Track
Rick Hansen — Track & Volleyball
Bill Inkster — Basketball
Leslie Lam — Track, Basketball & Table Tennis
Doug Lyons — Field & Weightlifting
Reg McClellan — Basketball
Ron Minor — Track & Basketball
Yvon Page — Shooting
Tom Parker — Archery
Eugene Reimer — Field & Basketball
Andre Viger — Track
Brian Ward — Archery
Don Warden — Archery

1984: NEW YORK, USA

Jaques Olivier — Minister of State, Fitnees and Amateur Sport

Chef de Mission — John Smyth
Amputee Team manager — Alan Dean
Blind Team manager — Gerry York
Disabled Games Chairman — Hugh Glynn
Disabled Games Officer — Chris Bowlby

Amputee Team

Asst Manager — Bob Wade
Technical Director — Patti Jones
Equipment Manager — Dale Murphy
Photographer — Madeleine Anderson
Escort — Gerry Sorenson
Coach — Karen Bashak
Coach — Jack Kelso

Athletes

Sheril Barrer — Track, Volleyball & Table Tennis
Staphania Balta — Field
Ann Farrell — Athletics & Volleyball
Josee Lake — Swimming

Joanne Mucz — Swimming
Jennifer Veenboer — Swimming
Magella Belanger — Track
Arnie Boldt — Field
Stephen Buell — Athletics
Tom Callahan — Athletics, Volleyball & Table Tennis
Lazlo Decsi — Pistol, Archery & Table Tennis
Ed Doerksen — Swimming
Ian Gregson — Field, Volleyball, Weightlifting
Angelo Gavillucci — Athletics
Mike Johnston — Field & Weightlifting
Sonny Lee — Table Tennis & Volleyball
Dan Leonard — Field & Volleyball
Don Locke — Swimming & Field
Mark Ludbrook — Swimming & Volleyball
Allison McNally — Athletics & Volleyball
Philip Mindorff — Swimming & Volleyball
Peter Palubicki — Field, Weightlifting & Volleyball
Denis Quenneville — Swimming
Angus Simpson — Swimming
Gary Simpson — Swimming & Volleyball
Jeff Tiessen — Athletics & Swimming
Ted Vince — Track
William Weibe — Athletics, Volleyball

Blind Team

Asst Team manager — Jane Arkell
Technical Advisor — Jim Leask
Physician — Dr Gordon Douglas
Official — Rene Ashton
Chaperon — Russ Sager
Escort — Garn York
Travel Co-Ordinator — Shirley Shelby
Interpreter — Robyn Hardie
Interpreter — Mike Ferras
Interpreter — Shelley Potts
Guide Runner — Rick Brant
Guide Runner — Sean Fitzgerald
Guide Runner — Tina Soubliere
Guide Runner — Mike York
Swim Tapper — Len Lear
Swim Tapper — Nancy Lear
Coach — Lorna Braden
Coach — Gary Gardiner
Coach — John Howe
Coach — Audrey Strom
Coach — Wilf Strom

Asst Coach — Jim Marvel
Asst Coach — Trish Rossi
Asst Coach — Louis Silviera
Asst Coach — Danny Snow

Athletes

Tami Boccaccio — Swimming
Maureen Ashton — Goalball
Lorraine Barnes — Track
Norah Good — Track
Cheryly Hurd — Track
Danielle Lessard — Goalball
Ljiliana Ljubisic — Goalball
Yvette Michel — Swimming
Christine Nicholas — Track
Andrea Rossi — Swimming
Chantal Rousseau — Goalball
Eva Sager — Goalball
Jacqueline Toews — Goalball
Kim Umbach — Track
Brian Arthur — Goalball
Tony Badger — Field
Rod Barkley — Track
Wayne Bell — Wrestling
Kenneth Booth — Swimming
Yvan Bourdeau — Athletics
Bill Cake — Swimming
Louis Deschenes — Track
Robert Deschenes — Goalball
Frank Di Pierdomenico — Wrestling
Dave Duncan — Wrestling
Mike Edgson — Swimming
Trent Fairbrother — Athletics
Bob Fenton — Swimming
Chris Gabriel — Swimming
Lee Grenon — Swimming
Scott Heron — Swimming
Gord Hope — Wrestling
Mark Hoyle — Swimming
Charles Kelly — Track
Kim Kilpatrick — Swimming
Bill Koch — Goalball
Pierre Lambert — Goalball
Andre Mainville — Track
Tim McIsaac — Swimming
Eddie Morten — Wrestling
Pier Morten — Wrestling
Keith Myette — Track

Jacques Pilon — Track
Rejean Poirier — Goalball
Wayne Prymych — Wrestling
Larry Rinke — Track
Matt Salli — Track
Dave Smith — Track
Bob Smith — Track
Greg Thompson — Swimming
Bruce Vandermolen — Swimming
Jim Visser — Swimming
Glen Wade — Goalball
Pat York — Track

1988: SEOUL, KOREA

Jean J. Charest — Minister of State Fitness and Amateur Sport

Chair CFSOD — Robert Steadward
CFSOD Executive Director — Anne Merklinger
Chef de Mission — Dick Loiselle
Team Attache — Mark Gwozdecky
Executive Assistant — Pat Heydon
Security Liason Officer — Don Wilson
Equipment Manager — Yvonne Hiney
Travel Coordinator — Zakaria Sheikh
Travel Coordinator — Jean Sheikh
Mission Secretary — Shirley King
Team Interpreter — Wei Nam Oh

Medical Staff
Chief Nedical Officer — Dr Michael Riding
Physician — Dr Emilie Newell
Physician — Dr Robert Burnham
Chief Therapist — Jim MacLeod
Therapist — Darren Booth
Therapist — Shayna Hornstein
Therapist — Elinor Houghton
Therapist — Glenn McPherson
Therapist — Jim Manzara
Physiotherapist — Rhonda Nishio
Prosthetist — Stan Holcomb
Nurse — Ena Hartel
Nurse — Charles Dyson

Communications
  Information Coordinator — Wendy Orr
  Photographer — Robert Peterson

Amputee Team

  Team Manager — Alan Dean
  Asst Team Manager — Dale Murphy
  Coach — Phil De Leeuw
  Coach — Norma Jordan
  Asst Coach — Karen Kvill
  Asst Coach — Robert Wade

Athletes
  John Belanger — Field
  Arnold Boldt — Field
  Lazlo Decsi — Shooting
  Jim Enright — Field
  Colin Farnan — Swimming
  Ian Gregson — Field
  Michael Johnston — Weightlifting
  Stephane Lecours — Swimming
  Sonny Lee — Table Tennis
  Mark Ludbrook — Swimming
  Philip Mindorff — Swimming
  Scott Patterson — Track
  Angus Simpson — Swimming
  Gary Simpson — Swimming
  Jeffrey Tiessen — Track
  Ted Vince — Track
  Daniel Westley — Track
  William Weibe — Track
  Linda Hamilton — Track
  Louise Henrioulle — Swimming
  Joanne Mucz — Swimming
  Claude Poumerol — Track
  Debbie Van Huizen — Track
  Lynette Wildman — Track

Blind Team

  Team Manager — Jim Leask
  Asst Team Manager — Jane Arkell
  Tapper — Cathy Arnold
  Coach — Lorna Braden
  Guide Runner — Barry Buchwald
  Coach — Raymond Cardinal
  Coach — Robert Dechenes
  Asst Coach — Tim Findlay

Asst Coach — Nicole Forget
Guide Runner — Edward Gillmor
Asst Coach — Colleen Heer
Support Staff — Gail Knudson
Coach — Tim Laidler
Intervenor — Jospeh Laing
Coach — Jim Marvel
Intervenor — Shelley Morten
Coach — Louis Silveira
Coach — Danny Snow
Coach — Wilfred Strom
Swim Tapper — Jane Thompson
Guide Runner — Kevin Waller

Athletes

Michelle Arnold — Swimming
Tamara Boccaccio — Swimming
Tammy Cole — Swimming
Patsy Campion — Goalball
Lucy Greco — Goalball
Danielle Lessard — Goalball
Ljiliana Ljubisic — Field
Tricia Lovegrove — Athletics
Lisa McLeod — Goalball
Christine Nicholas — Athletics
Carla Qualtrough — Swimming
Diane Robitaille — Swimming
Helena Rooyakkers — Goalball
Jacqueline Toews — Field
Yvette Weicker — Swimming
Tony Badger — Goallball
Ken Bjorn — Swimming
Camilien Boudreau — Track
Yvan Boudreau — Athletics
Mario Caron — Goalball
Gene Della Siega — Athletics
Louis Deschenes — Track
Francois Dupere — Judo
Mike Edgson — Swimming
Trent Fairbrother — Goalball
Robert Gaunt — Goalball
Lee Grenon — Swimming
Scott Herron — Swimming
Kevin Kaminski-Morris — Goalball
Tim McIsaac — Swimming
Eddie Morten — Judo
Pier Morten — Judo

Keith Myette — Track
Patrick Page — Athletics
Adrian Peirson — Swimming
Harry Pierre-Etienne — Judo
Shepsell Shell — Marathon
Robert Smith — Track
Patrick York — Track
Mark Zillman — Track

Cerebral Palsy Team

Team Manager — Doug Wilton
Coach — Janet Dunn
Asst Coach — Manon Gregorie
Coach — Keith Hanson
Coach — Leona Holland
Coach — Tom Landry
Support Staff — Lauri Miller
Support Staff — Anna Misciangna
Support Staff — Garnet Robinson
Coach — Carrie Riddle
Coach — John Ritchie

Athletes

Sonja Atkins — Track
Tammy Barker — Swimming
Sylvie Bergeron — Track
Halldor Bjarnason — Cycling
James Bone — Track
Joanne Bouw — Field
Dean Dwyer — Cycling
Susan Chick — Swimming
Robert Easton — Track
Judy Goodrich — Swimming
Rick Gronman — Field
Raquel Head — Track
Joe Higgins — Swimming
David Howe — Athletics
Michael Johner — Track
Gilles Lafrance — Track
Andre Lavallee — Track
Gary Longhi — Cycling
Norma Lorincz — Track
Marjorie Lynch — Track
Robert Mearns — Track
Laura Misciagna — Track
Terry Robinson — Athletics & Boccia
Sylvie Sauve — Track

David Severin — Track
Ken Thomas — Track
Gino Vendetti — Track
Brent Warner — Track
Debbie Willows — Athletics & Boccia
Jeff Worobetz — Swimming

Wheelchair Team

Team Manager — Lori Crosby
Asst Team Manager — Frank MacIntyre
Coach — Steve Bach
Asst Coach — Guy Berthiaume
Asst Coach — Gilles Boulley
Equipment Manager — Larry Dobson
Equipment Manager — Yves Julien
Coach — Charles Drouin
Asst Coach — Mari Ellery
Coach — Brent Foster
Coach — Henriette Groeneveld
Coach — Jean Laroche
Coach — Finn Peterson
Technical Coordinator — Dr Donald Royer
Coach — Alex Cranfield Sinclair
Asst Coach — Garry Smith

Athletes

Jeffrey Adams — Track
Alain Baillargeon — Marathon
Andre Beaudoin — Track
Chantal Benoit — Basketball
Murray Brown — Basketball
Paul Clark — Track
Adrienne Colby — Swimming
Erick Corsaut — Basketball
Christopher Daw — Track
Alec Denys — Archery
Diane Earl — Basketball
Elaine Ell — Basketball
Robert Ellery — Track
Kevin Gardiner — Track
Bernard Gehring — Shooting
Clayton Gerein — Track
Luke Gingras — Marathon
Patrick Griffin — Basketball
Doug Grant — Marathon
Matha Gustafson — Track
Roy Henderson — Basketball

Braden Hirsch — Basketball
Darlene Jackman — Basketball
Paul Johnson — Track
Debbie Kostelyk — Track
Linda Kutrowski — Basketball
Heather Kuttai — Air Pistol
Denis Lapalme — Basketball
David Lash — Track
Nicole Leboeuf — Basketball
Glenn Mariash — Shooting
Jacques Martin — Field
John May — Basketball
Helga McKay — Track
Stewart McKeown — Field
Ron Minor — Basketball
Jeffrey Penner — Basketball
Diane Pidskalny-Hrychuk — Basketball
Marc Quessy — Marathon
Diane Rakiecki — Track
Serge Raymond — Marathon
Richard Reelie — Field
Ron Scanlan — Track
Bruce Russell — Basketball
Adam Salamandyk — Shooting
Tami Saj — Swimming
Christopher Samis — Basketball
Gary Schaff — Field
Richard Schell — Shooting
Donna Shaw — Basketball
Tham Simpson — Track
Marney St Louis — Basketball
Daryl Stubel — Track
Roxanne Ulanicki — Basketball
Andre Viger — Track
Mary Jan Waugh — Basketball
Irene Wownuk — Basketball
Randall Wyness — Basketball
Judy Zelman — Field

1996: ATLANTA, USA

Note: Athletes are now organized by sport, not disability

Sheila Copps — Minister of Canadian Heritage

Chef de Mission — Karen O' Niell

Sport Coordinators
Ross Bales
Ollie Currie
Patrick Jarvis
Sharron St Croix
Brian Skinner
Doug Wilton

Medical Staff
Dr Susan Labrecque
John Boulay
Dr Douglas Dittmer
Jane Drouin
Bob Dunlop
Raymonde Fortin
Doug Freer
Wendy hampson
James Bilotta
Lorette Madore
Nancy Quinn

Support Staff
Don Alder
Ray Allard
Ce Ce Cubitt
Pat Heydon
Keith Hobbs
Mary Jane King
Daniel Normandine
Aline Lafreniere
Ann Peel
Carla Qualtrough
Zak Sheikh
Jane Shiekh
Ron Thompson

Archery

Alec Denys
Arthur Nault

Athletics

Jeff Adams
Andre Beaudoin
Dean Bergeron
Jacques Bouchard
Frank Bruno
John Bunz
Nick Cunningham
Jason Delesalle
Steve Ellefson
France Gagne
Clayton Gerein
Rick Gronman
David Howe
Jason Lachance
Carl Marquis
Jacques Martin
Colin Mathieson
Stuart McGregor
Brent McMahon
Hal Merrill
Marc Quessy
Joey Radmore
Rick Reelie
James Reilly
Johnathon Rowell
James Shaw
Robert Snoek
Dominque Tremblay
Andre Viger
Collette Bourgonje
Joanne Bouw
Linda Hamilton
Kris Hodjkins
Courtney Knight
Ljiljana Ljubisic
Kristine Lucas
Tracey Melesko
Chantal Peticlerc
Diane Roy
Charmaine Shand

Coaches

Faye Blackwood
Earl Church
Anthony Clegg
Peter Eriksson
Jean Laroche
Robert Schrader
Don Steen
Norma Suarez-Jordan

Basketball

Jaimie Borisoff
Dan Brinton
Erick Corsaut
David Durepos
Jim Enright
Pat Griffin
Ken Hall
Roy Henderson
Joe Johnson
Stewart McKeown
Richard Peter
James Treuer
Marni Abbott
Chantal Benoit
Renee DelColle
Tracey Ferguson
Jennifer Kremplin
Kelly Krywa
Linda Kutrowski
Kendra Ohama
Sabrina Pettinicchi
Lori Radke
Marney Smithies
Lisa Stevens

Coaches

Paul Bowes
Tim Frick
Mike Frogley
Barb Griffin
Joe Higgins
Jerry Tonello
Paul Zachau

Boccia

Francois Bourbonniere
Wayne Collins
Clarence Doucette
Paul Gauthier
Nathalie Menard
Stefan Putnam
Peter Brown
Terry Robinson

Directors

Noreen Guptill
Patricia Hayes
Jennifer Larson
Martin Paul
Albert Punzalan
Derek Wyse
Lyn Robinson

Cycling

Patrice Bonneau
Julie Cournoyer
Gary Longhi
Carla Yustak

Coach

Stephane Cote
Eric van den Eynde

Pilots

Alexandre Cloutier
Guylaine Larouche

Equestrian Events

Gregory Honour
Karine Meador
Marnie Payne
Maria Simpson

Staff

Jane James
Wendy Roberts
Nancy Tapley
Jo Young

Goalball

Mario Caron
Jean-Francois Crepault
Robert Gaunt
Eric Houle
Dean Kozak

Coaches

Robert Deschenes
Launel Scott

Judo

Pier Morten

Coach

Savas Iydogan

Intervenor

Shelly Morten

Lawn Bowling

Howard Cordick
Bob Giesbrecht
Al Hanet
Lance McDonald
Ed McMillan
Ron Pelletier
Vivian Berkeley
Peggy Casey
Leslie Sadd
Elaine Smithson

Directors

Shirley Ahern
Eric Ferguson
Barb Giesbrecht
Vi Hanet
Don Mayne
Florence McClellan
Roy Sadd
Don Sherry
Walter Shopka
Gord Watson

Powerlifting

Ken Doyle
Steven Stewart
Andrew Wrzeszcz

Coach
Frank Quinn

Rugby

Mike Bacon
Dany Belanger
Garett Hickling
Kirby Kranabetter
Raymond Lizotte
Brian McPhate
Al Semeniuk
Daryl Stubel

Coaches
Mark Maillet
Mardy Rust

Shooting

Laszlo Decsi
Bruce Heidt
Mike Larochelle
Glenn Mariash
Chris Trifondis

Coaches
Bob Kierstead
Jack Ramsey

Swimming

Tony Alexander
Benny Galati
Jeremy Gervan
Andrew Haley
Garth Harris
Jamie Johnston
Robert Penner
Adam Purdy
Walter Wu
Rebeccah Bornemann
Joelle Rivard
Marie Claire Ross

Elisabeth Walker

Coach
Bill Greenlaw
Tristan Johnson

Tennis

Paul Johnson
Mario Perron

Coach
Barry Bruce

Yachting

David Cook
Ken Kelly
John McRoberts
Kirk Westergaard

Coach
Cindy Sheppard

The Triumphant Return of Canada's First Paralympic Team

Vancouver Sun   November 1968

by Denny Boyd

They cleared customs and they went up the ramp to the waiting room, hands pumping at the wheels, and on the back of each wheelchair was a maroon flag that said "Canada."

Gene Reimer's two little boys came barrelling down the corridor and each of them was holding a sign that said, "My Dad won a gold medal for me." They jumped on him and there was a whole bunch of mush and stuff because their Dad had been away for two weeks.

All of them were bone-weary because they had been airborne for 23 hours and when you are a paraplegic you don't get up and walk around an awful lot. Besides that, there was a bit of a sweat over the Uzo, a Greek liquor that some of them had cunningly stuffed into their baggage.

Canada's Paralympic team was back.

There were perhaps 300 people at Vancouver's International Airport and they were waving banners that said, "Welcome Home, Big Wheels." That's an inside joke that causes wheelchair types to break up. The Parks Board was represented by George Puil and the Provincial Government by Grace McCarthy. As well, virtually every member of the Little Lower Academy student body was there and they had a 16-foot long banner welcoming their schoolmate, Karen McPherson, who had won a silver and two bronze medals at the recent Paralympics in Israel.

If the BC members of the Canadian Paralympic team were a bit overweight in their luggage, it could be ascribed to two factors: the Uzo, and the fact that they were packing a bunch of medals. To be precise, the Canadian Team in the "wheelchair Olympics," as it is called, won six gold medals, six silvers and seven bronzes. British Columbia members of the team accounted for five of the gold, two of the silver and four of the bronze.

By the time Gene Reimer peeled the kids off, he was able to show the two golds and the silver he had won. He got the golds in the discus and the club throw and he set world records in both events. It has been 17 years since someone thought to start recording the athletic efforts of people who live in wheelchairs and I think we should all stand a little straighter today with pride in what Reimer has done.

Doug Wilson was pretty well-heeled, too. He had two gold medals and a pack of stories about the trip. Wilson looks a bit like Tab Hunter and he has been wheelchair bound since an under-aged, non-licensed driver of a car with no insurance knocked Doug off his bike.

Team manager Doug Mowatt remembered most vividly the basketball game between Canada and the host Israeli team. "Back about 1953, they had a pretty bad outbreak of polio over there and some of the victims are starting to come of athletic age. They had been prepping for this game for about two years and they had just a fantastic team. When we played them, there were about 3,000 people in the stands, including Moishe Dayan, and they turned thousands away because they just didn't have the seats. Well, it was one hell of a basketball game, but they had us all the way. But I'll never forget the sound of that crowd, chanting 'El, el, Israel.' And when one of our guys went in for a free throw, the crowd would start a low whistle that rose to a crescendo and it just about split your ears."

And now it's time for the commercial: This team of Wilson, Reimer, Karen McPherson, Glendine (Snooky) Seely, Lorna Vinden, Walter Schmid, Gunther Schuster, Dick Wasnock and Mel Hamilton, together with manager Mowatt and Vic Cue, put up $200 apiece and signed a bank note for $3,000 for the privilege of competing in Tel Aviv for Canada.

We have a drive going here for the purpose of paying off their bills. We have $1,500 so far and we need more. If you want to share that gold medal that Gene Reimer won for his kids, send in a donation or a cheque payable to me or to the BC Wheelchair Sports and Recreation Association. I know some tired, proud guys in wheelchairs who would appreciate it.

CONTACT INFORMATION FOR DISABILITY SPORTS ORGANIZATIONS

INTERNATIONAL DISABILITY SPORT ORGANIZATIONS

International Wheelchair Tennis Federation (IWTF)

Palliser Road, Barons Court
London W14 9EN
TEL: 44 171 381 8060; FAX: 44 171 381 3989
e-mail: itf@itftennis.com

NATIONAL DISABILITY SPORT ORGANIZATIONS

Canadian Amputee Sports Association

428 Lake Bonavista Dr. S.E.,Calgary,T2J 0M1
TEL: (403) 278-8772; FAX: (403) 271-1920
ampsport@interlog.com
http://www.interlog.com/~ampsport/can_amputee.html

Canadian Association for Disabled Skiing

PO Box 307, 2860 Rotary Dr., Kimberley, V1A 1E9
TEL: (604) 427-7712; FAX: (604) 427-7715
http://www.canuck.com/cads/
balfour@canuck.com

Canadian Blind Sports Association

1600 James Naismith Dr., Suite 606A, Gloucester, K1B 5N4
TEL: (613) 748-5609; FAX: (613) 748-5731

Canadian Cerebral Palsy Sports Association (CCPSA), Head Office

1600 James Naismith Drive
Gloucester, Ontario
K1B 5N4
TEL: (613) 748-5725; FAX: (613) 748-5899
e-mail: chill@rtm.cdnsport.ca

Canadian Deaf Ice Hockey Federation

1650 Lewes Way, Mississauga, L4W 3L2
TEL: (905) 624-7494; FAX: (905) 624-6770
rhysen@onramp.ca
http://home.interlynx.net/~relacis/cdihf.htm

Canadian Deaf Sports Association

1367 W. Broadway, Suite 218, Vancouver, V6H 4A9
TEL: (604) 737-3041; FAX: (604) 738-7175

Canadian Deaf Volleyball

TEL: (705) 322-1688; TTY: (705) 322-0258; FAX: (705) 322-2245
mpersi@bconnex.net

Canadian Paralympic Committee

1600 James Naismith Dr., Gloucester, K1B 5N4
TEL: (613) 748-5630; FAX: (613) 748-5731
http://paralympic.ca/
cpc@paralympic.ca

Canadian Special Olympics

40 St Clair Ave. W., Suite 209, Toronto, M4V 1M2
TEL: (416) 927-9050; FAX: (416) 927-8475
solympic@inforamp.net

Canadian Wheelchair Basketball Association

1600 James Naismith Dr., Suite 715, Gloucester, K1B 5N4
TEL: (613) 748-5888; FAX: (613) 748-5889
cwba@cwba.ca
http://www.cwba.ca/

Canadian Wheelchair Sports Association

1600 James Naismith Dr., Suite 212A, Gloucester, K1B 5N4
TEL: (613) 748-5685; FAX: (613) 748-5722
http://indie.ca/cwsa/
cwsa@bpg.ca

National Capital Handicapped Ski Association

RR #2, Wakefield, J0X 3G0
TEL: (819) 459-2714

National Capital Sports Council of the Disabled Inc.

D.P.C.R., 1525 Carling Ave., Lower level, Ottawa, K1Z 8R9
TEL: (613) 724-1115
http://www.magma.ca/~ncscd/
council@ncscd.ca

Team Canada Disabled Volleyball

tcdv@cadvision.com
http://www.cadvision.com/Home_Pages/accounts/tcdv/

Provincial & Territorial Disability Sport Associations

ALBERTA

Alberta Deaf Sports Association

PO Box 11741, Edmonton, T5J 3K8
TEL: (403) 438-8079; FAX: (403) 438-9114

Alberta Sports & Recreation Association for the Blind
PO Box 85056, Albert Park, Calgary, T2A 7R7
TEL: (403) 262-5332; FAX: (403) 265-7221

Alberta Therapeutic Riding Association

PO Box 1191, Carstairs, T0M 0N0
TEL: (403) 337-2950

Canadian Special Olympics - Alberta

11759 Groat Rd., Edmonton, T5M 3K6
TEL: (403) 453-8520; FAX: (403) 453-8553
solympic@inforamp.net

Canadian Therapeutic Riding Association - Zone 2

1205 - 8th St. N., Lethbridge, T1H 1Z3
TEL: (403) 327-9182

Paralympic Sports Association

10426 - 81st. Ave., Edmonton, T6E 1X5
TEL: (403) 439-8687

BRITISH COLUMBIA

British Columbia Blind Sports & Recreation Association

1367 W. Broadway, Suite 317, Vancouver, V6H 4A9
TEL: (604) 325-1638; FAX: (604) 325-1638

British Columbia Deaf Sport Federation

1367 W. Broadway, Suite 218, Vancouver, V6H 4A9
TEL: (604) 737-3041   TDD (604) 783-7122,

British Columbia Therapeutic Riding Association

11513 Tassle Dr., Vernon, V1B 1H3
TEL: (604) 542-9816; FAX: (604) 542-5116

Canadian Special Olympics - British Columbia

1367 West Broadway, Suite 226, Vancouver, V6H 4A9
TEL: (604) 737-3078; FAX: (604) 737-6043
solympic@inforamp.net

Disabled Sailing Association of B.C.

(Chapters in Vancouver, Victoria, Kelowna, & Penticton)
Box 27, 770 Pacific Blvd., South Vancouver, V6B 5E7
TEL: (604) 688-6464; FAX: (604) 688-6463
dsa@reachdisability.org (email)
www.reachdisability.org/dsa (website)

MANITOBA

Canadian Special Olympics - Manitoba

200 Main St., 4th Floor, Winnipeg, R3C 4M2
TEL: (204) 925-5628   (204) 925-5635
solympic@inforamp.net

Canadian Therapeutic Riding Association - Zone 3

RR #1, Headingley, R0H 0J0
TEL: (204) 895-4310

Manitoba Deaf Sports Association

285 Pembina Hwy., Suite 322, Winnipeg, R3L 2E1
TEL: (204) 632-1166

Manitoba Therapeutic Riding Association

One Lombard Pl., Suite1313, Winnipeg, R3B 0X3
TEL: (204) 956-1282

Manitoba Wheelchair Sport & Recreation Association Inc.

1495 St. Matthews, Winnipeg, R3G 3L3
TEL: (204) 985-4145

Sport & Recreation Association for the Blind

1700 Ellice Ave., Winnipeg, R3H 0B1
TEL: (204) 786-5641

NEW BRUNSWICK

Canadian Special Olympics - New Brunswick

461 King St., Fredericton, E3B 1E5
TEL: (506) 459-3999; FAX: (506) 453-1768

Fredericton Therapeutic Riding Association

90 Waterloo Row, Fredericton, E3B 1Y9
TEL: (506) 455-0510; FAX: (506) 452-2729

Greater Moncton Riding for the Disabled

Horizon Farm, RR #3, Moncton, E1C 8J7
TEL: (506) 386-5383
solympic@inforamp.net

New Brunswick Blind Sports Association

80 Riverside Dr., Fredericton, E3A 3Y1
TEL: (506) 472-5941

New Brunswick Deaf Sports Association

65 Brunswick St., Suite 902, Fredericton, E3B 1G5
TEL: (506) 642-3903

NOVA SCOTIA

Antigonish Therapeutic Riding Association

RR #3, Malignant Cove, Antigonish County, B2G 2L1
TEL: (902) 863-2018

Blind Sports Nova Scotia

PO Box 31186, Robie PRO, Halifax , B3K 5Y1
TEL: (902) 453-1480, ext. 146

Canadian Therapeutic Riding Association - Zone 6

RR #2, Burnside Farm, Amherst, B4H 3X9
TEL: (902) 667-9908; FAX: (902) 667-0155

Central Therapeutic Riding Association

180A Main St., Truro, B2N 4H2
TEL: (902) 895-3750

Deaf Sports Nova Scotia

PO Box 20030, Halifax , B3R 2K9
Nova Scotia Riding for the Disabled Association
RR #2, Three Fathom Harbour, Halifax County, B0U 1N0
TEL: (902) 827-3053

PRINCE EDWARD ISLAND

Canadian Special Olympics - PEI

PO Box 841, 3 Queen St., Suite 119, Charlottetown, C1A 7L9
TEL: (902) 368-4543; FAX: (902) 368-4542
solympic@inforamp.net

Joyriders Therapeutic Riding Association of P.E.I.

PO Box 1904, Charlottetown, C1A 7N5
TEL: (902) 892-3790

Prince Edward Island Recreation & Sports Association for the Physically Challenged

PO Box 841, Charlottetown, C1A 7L9
TEL: (902) 892-5363

Prince Edward Island Wheelchair Sports Association

PO Box 841, Charlottetown, C1A 7L9
TEL: (902) 368-4540

NEWFOUNDLAND

Canadian Special Olympics - Newfoundland

PO Box 2584, 210 Water St., Suite 300, Station C,
St.John's, A1C 6K1
TEL: (709) 738-1923   (709) 738-0119
solympic@inforamp.net

Newfoundland Deaf Sports Association

PO Box 9125, Stn. J, Mount Pearl, A1A 2X3
TEL: (709) 576-4592

St. John's Therapeutic Riding Association

PO Box 9236, 139 Portugal Cove Rd.,
St. John's, A1A 2X9
TEL: (709) 753-3229

ONTARIO

Adult Disabled Downhill Skiers

91 Gayla St., Thornhill, L3T 3J2
TEL: (905) 660-0047

Canadian Deaf Sports Association

Canadian Sports & Fitness Administration Centre,
1600 James Naismith Dr., Ottawa, K1B 5N4
TEL: (613) 748-5789; TTD (613) 748-5736; FAX: (613) 748-5736

Canadian Special Olympics - Ontario

1185 Eglinton Ave. E., Suite 503, North York, M3C 3C6
TEL: (416) 426-7277 and 1-888-333-5515; FAX: (416) 426-7341
solympic@inforamp.net

Canadian Therapeutic Riding Association

PO Box 1055, Guelph, N1H 6J6
TEL: (519) 767-0700

Canadian Therapeutic Riding Association - Zone 4

PO Box 1434, 148 Union St., Almonte, K0A 1A0
TEL: (613) 256-4554

Central Ontario Developmental Riding Program

584 Pioneer Tower Rd., Kitchener, N2G 3W6
TEL: (519) 653-4686

Cruisers Sports Club for the Disabled of Halton Peel

1184 Flagship Dr., Mississauga, L4Y 2K1

Durham Region Horseback Riding for the Handicapped Association

PO Box 24, Blackstock, L0B 1B0
TEL: (905) 986-5558

Ontario Blind Curlers Association

569 Maple Ave., Sudbury, P3C 2B8
TEL: (705) 673-8812

Ontario Blind Sports Association

1220 Sheppard Ave. E., Suite 104, Willowdale, M2K 2X1
TEL: (416) 495-4163; FAX: (416) 495-4135

Ontario Deaf Curling Association

21 Midland Cr., Suite 56, Nepean, K2H 8P6
TEL: (613) 828-8199

Ontario Deaf Sports Association

502 Essa Rd., Apt. 13, Barrie, L4M 4S7

Ontario Theapeutic Riding Association

1308 Redwood Lane, Pickering, L1X 1C5
TEL: (905) 446-3050

Southern Ontario Deaf Skiers Association

5070 Dixie Rd., Mississauga, L4W 1C9
TEL: (905) 629-5094

QUEBEC

Association regionale de loisir pour personnes handicapées - Est du Quebec

RR #1320, CP 69, Ste-Luce, G0K 1P0
TEL: (418) 739-4990; FAX: (418) 739-4865

Canadian Special Olympics - Québec

5 Place Ville Marie, Suite 1440, Montréal, H3B 2G2
TEL: (514) 878-0939; FAX: (514) 878-4789
solympic@inforamp.net

Fédération des loisirs & sports pour handicapés du Québec

4545, av. Pierre-de-Coubertin, CP 1000, succ. M,
Montréal, H1V 3R2
TEL: (514) 252-3000

Fondation de thérapie équestre - Les Nouveaux Écuyers

3575, rue St-Laurent, bureau 905, Montréal, H2X 2T7
TEL: (514) 767-3937; FAX: (514) 848-0365

Recreation for the Handicapped Inc.

1800 Réné Lévesque Blvd. W., Suite 22, Montréal, H3H 2H2
TEL: (514) 935-1109

YWCA Recreational Programmes for Handicapped

1355 Réné Lévesque Blvd. W., Suite 116, Montréal, H3G 1T3
TEL: (514) 866-9941

SASKATCHEWAN

Battlefords Therapeutic Riding Association

PO Box 1328, North Battleford, S9A 3L8
TEL: (306) 445-3381

Canadian Special Olympics - Saskatchewan

353 Broad St., Regina, S4R 1X2
TEL: (306) 780-9247   (306) 780-944
solympic@inforamp.net

Handicapped Integrated Riders of the South West

PO Box 182, Swift Current, S9H 3V6
TEL: (306) 773-7728

Saskatchewan Therapeutic Riding Association

PO Box 2151, Moose Jaw, S6H 7T2
TEL: (306)693-2282   ; FAX: (306) 694-2021

Saskatoon Horses & the Handicapped Inc.

RR #4, PO Box 607, Saskatoon, S7K 3J7
TEL: (306) 242-6766

Southcentral Handicap Integrated Riding Association

PO Box 1641, Moose Jaw, S6H 7K7
TEL: (306) 694-4102

INDEX OF PEOPLE AND ORGANIZATIONS

PHOTO CREDITS

Cover photographs used with the kind permission of Canadian Sport Images (wheelchair basketball) and F. Scott Grant Photography and Swim Canada (swimmer).

The following interior photographs are used courtesy of the author, Ian Gregson: p. 17; p. 23; p. 26; p. 28; p. 37; p. 45; p. 58; p. 61; p. 62; p. 68; p. 74; p. 77; p. 80; p. 85; p.87; p. 94; p. 96; p. 100; p. 101; p. 103; p. 109; p. 110; p. 111; p. 112; p. 113

Other photographs are used with the kind permission of the following people and organizations:
p. 22: courtesy Edward Mathiso
p. 30 (both photographs): courtesy CBSA
p. 34: courtesy CBSA
p. 39: courtesy Mike Armstrong
p. 42: courtesy Bonnie Blacklock, Recreation Integration Victoria
p. 47: courtesy Alain Joly
p. 49: courtesy Nellie Bos
p. 52: photo by F. Scott Grant Photography; courtesy Swim Canada
p. 56: photo by Dan Galbraith, Disability Today Publishing; courtesy Swim Canada
p. 59: photo by Claus Andersen; courtesy Canadian Sport Images
p. 64: courtesy CBSA
p. 66: photo by Claus Andersen; courtesy Canadian Sport Images
p. 69: photo by Christine Chew; courtesy Canadian Sport Images
p. 75: courtesy Alberta Northern Lights Wheelchair Basketball Society
p. 76: courtesy Alberta Northern Lights Wheelchair Basketball Society
p. 90: (all three photographs) courtesy CBSA

About the Author

Ian Gregson grew up in Lancashire, England where he excelled in athletics. When he was fourteen, he lost his right leg in an accident. He moved to British Columbia, Canada in 1981 and completed a degree at Simon Fraser University in Vancouver, where he was the first Canadian athlete with a disability to be given a university athletic scholarship. Over the years he has participated in numerous Paralympic events. He now sits on the boards of the BC Coalition of People with Disabilities and the Gordie Howe Disabled Athletes Foundation. He also produces *Amputee Home Page* and *Amputation Online Magazine*. Ian Gregson lives in Vancouver, BC.

BRIGHT LIGHTS FROM POLESTAR BOOK PUBLISHERS

Polestar takes pride in creating books that enrich our understanding of the world and introduce discriminating readers to exciting writers. Here are some of our best-selling sports titles.

Celebrating Excellence: Canadian Women Athletes
Wendy Long
A collection of biographical essays and photos that showcases more than 200 female athletes who have achieved excellence.
1-896095-04-6 • $29.95 CDN/$24.95 USA

Behind the Mask, revised edition
Ian Young and Chris Gudgeon
Here is every goaltender's essential handbook, including physical and psychological techniques and game-action photos.
1-896095-51-8 • $18.95 CDN/$14.95 USA

Home Run: A Modern Approach to Baseball Skill Building
Michael McRae
Skills specialist McRae offers a solid base of technical instruction for players and coaches who are learning and teaching baseball fundamentals.
1-896095-29-1 • $18.95 CDN/$15.95 USA

Long Shot: Steve Nash's Journey to the NBA
Jeff Rud
Profile of young NBA star Steve Nash, detailing the determination and skill that carried him through high school and college basketball into the ranks of the pros.
1-896095-16-x • $18.95 CDN/$16.95 USA

Our Game: A Collection of All-Star Hockey Fiction
Doug Beardsley, editor
From the Forum to the backyard rink, this collection of 30 stories illuminates the essence of the hockey soul.
1-896095-26-7 • $18.95 CDN/$16.95 USA

Skywalking: How 10 Young Basketball Stars Soared to the Pros
Jeff Rud
Inspiring profiles of today's hottest young basketball stars and their unconventional paths to the big leagues.
1-896095-46-1 • $18.95 CDN/$15.95 USA

Too Many Men on the Ice: Women's Hockey in North America
Joanna Avery and Julie Stevens
A fascinating look at all levels of women's hockey in Canada and the United States, including in-depth profiles of prominent players.
1-896095-33-x • $19.95 CDN/$16.95 USA

Polestar titles are available from your local bookseller. For a copy of our catalogue, contact:
POLESTAR BOOK PULISHERS
103-1014 Homer Street
Vancouver, BC
Canada V6B 2W9
mypage.direct.ca/p/polestar